CROCHET—PRETTY AND PRACTICAL

By the same author:

Fashion Crochet
Fashion Crochet for your Doll

Crochet – Pretty & Practical

Caroline Horne

MILLS & BOON LIMITED,
LONDON

First published in Great Britain 1973 by
Mills & Boon Limited,
17–19 Foley Street, London W1A 1DR

ISBN 0 263.05151.X

Printed in Great Britain by Butler & Tanner Limited
Frome and London

Contents

Acknowledgements

The illustrations of stitches in *Crochet—Pretty and Practical* were taken from the Coats Sewing Group Book *Crochet Stitches*. I am most grateful to J. and P. Coats for allowing me to use these illustrations.

I would like to thank Mrs Peggy Band late of Hampton-in-Arden, Warwickshire, a teacher in pewter work for the Warwickshire Federation of Women's Institutes, for making the pewter frame for the picture tray on page 114.

List of Abbreviations

ch.	=	chain
sl. st.	=	slip stitch
dc.	=	double crochet
hlf. tr	=	half treble
tr.	=	treble
dbl. tr.	=	double treble
st.	=	stitch
grp.	=	group
hlf. grp.	=	half group
tr. grp.	=	treble group
sp.	=	space
blk.	=	block
inc.	=	increase
dec.	=	decrease
*	=	repeat the instructions following as many times as specified in addition to the original.
( )	=	when these are used to show repetition, work directions as many times as specified. i.e., (2 tr., 2 ch., 2 tr.) 3 times, means do what is in ( ) 3 times altogether.
w.o.h	=	wool over hook

Introduction

Crochet—Pretty and Practical contains quite a selection of crochet ideas. There are simple sleeveless blouses, suits, a beautiful wedding dress and there is also a variety of practical items for the home. The stitch patterns range from simple ones for beginners, working up to patterns a little more difficult—but by no means complicated—for the more advanced worker. These are mostly a permutation of the treble stitch.

It is quite rightly said that the treble is the most popular stitch in crochet and to the creative mind there is no limit to the designs which can be produced from it—one can sit and 'doodle' with a crochet hook, a ball of wool and a treble and find oneself making a diversity of patterns from this one stitch. Also a 'rhythm' flows along a row of mixed trebles which is missing when a complicated design is being worked.

I have tried—especially for the garments—to aim at simplicity in stitch patterns to make up into useful as well as attractive wearing apparel. The easy to work garments for the beginner are:

Sleeveless cotton blouse: A very easy 3-tr. group pattern, a change from crocheting squares and without all the seemingly endless ends to darn in.

Nightdress yoke: Useful and quickly made—also pleasing made up in your own choice of colours.

Working up from the very easy:

Tabard: This is worked in 'Twisted tr.'—a simple stitch with a different look. The tabard is a change from a sleeveless cardigan and a useful addition to any wardrobe. Worn with trousers and blouse it can look quite attractive with or without the fringe.

Ribbed Skirt: A useful skirt using another type of trs.—'raised and depressed'. Simple and quickly worked and very effective with stripes of bright colours. The stripes can be worked in widths to

your own liking or, alternatively, these can be omitted for a plain
skirt to team up with any colour blouse or jumper.

Working a little further up the scale towards advanced crochet:

Suit with raglan sleeves: This is really quite easy to make, the
raglan sleeves fitting in perfectly with the pattern on fronts and
back of coat. The mitred borders give an added interest.

Shirtwaister dress: A mixed treble stitch is used for this very useful
dress which in my opinion is another 'must' for the wardrobe.
With a scarf tucked in at the neck it is just the thing for morning,
afternoon or casual evening wear.

Chanel-type suit: This is worked in the same stitch pattern as the
shirtwaister which gives attractive fabric crochet and is for the
more advanced worker. The blouse to team up with the suit is in
a 3-tr. cluster st. with the spots in dc. A suit one would feel 'right'
in on any occasion.

Wedding dress: With a special stitch for a special occasion. The
bodice part of the dress is easy—just ordinary tr. and twin tr. but
the lacy part of the skirt is quite different from any basic crochet
sts.

Some women tend to read a pattern before trying it out and think
'Oh, this is too difficult' and immediately discard it. Personally,
I think this is a mistake, so don't begin to read this pattern
without a crochet hook and a ball of wool in your hand—work
the pattern as you read and once you have the rhythm of the
stitch, you will find it quite easy.

As this dress begins at the neck and is worked downwards, the
pattern can be adapted for a short-sleeved cocktail dress or a
sleeveless evening dress. A dinner gown with this pattern and using
Sirdar 'After Six' or Lister's 'Star-Spun' would be excellent.
Jaeger's 'Dappel Crepe Courtelle' can also be used for this
pattern.

Before embarking on this project—a fair-sized practice piece of the lace design should be worked to obtain a good tension.

Christening gown and coat: After the wedding dress, what better garment with which to end this part of the book—the pattern being the same stitch as the wedding dress.

Now, a reminder—and this is essential. Before attempting to make any of these garments—check your tension. A large-sized practice piece should be worked with the wool or yarn and crochet hook specified in the pattern for, unlike knitting, crochet expands with the first few rows and gradually 'takes up' as the work grows.

Crochet for the home
In the district in which I live, I come across women who still like to keep a 'bit of cotton crochet on the go' and something that is 'quickly done'. I think perhaps there may be women elsewhere who feel the same, so, I have compiled a few patterns of useful articles which are quickly worked and will—I hope—be pleasing to the eye.

Bedspreads: These are very attractive when finished and really 'make the bed'. Made in thick cotton, the squares are quickly made and not in the least laborious.

Cushion cover: This can look more colourful by using oddments of wool for the centres.

Plate doily: Very useful and attractive when friends drop in for coffee and colourful as a wall plate—will match up with the finger plate.

Penguin finger plate will fit in either the bathroom or nursery.

The tray with pewter frame will be useful for wine glasses or will give a pleasing effect as a picture.

Types and quantities of yarn
With crochet patterns, as with knitting, there is always the problem that the reader may not be able to find the exact yarn

specified—or may simply prefer to use something a little different.
At this present time, there is the extra complication that we are
'going metric', and that manufacturers (in the USA as well as in
UK are packing many of their products in balls that are classified
by the gram rather than the ounce. Further differences arise if one
prefers to use a blend of wool and synthetic yarn, as these may
be packed into either a 20-gram or a 25-gram ball, depending on
the proportion of pure wool to synthetic used in the processing.

Consequently, at the beginning of each pattern I have specified the
yarn I actually used, and have also suggested alternatives. These
I hope will work well in practice. It will be noted that for some
of the larger sizes, where extra groups are recommended in
brackets, one or two more balls of yarn will be needed.

Adjusting patterns for different measurements

To make a jumper or dress larger or smaller than given in directions, i.e. 38-inch to 40-inch bust size, or 36-inch to 34-inch bust size, add or subtract the number of stitches or patterns equalling 1 inch to both back and front.

For coat: 1 inch to back and $\frac{1}{2}$ inch to each front.

For skirt: 2 inches (1 inch to each back and front).

To obtain width desired at shoulders, decrease more or less stitches at armhole shaping, decreasing stitches equally at each armhole.

Under-arm of sleeve: For a larger size, add $\frac{1}{2}$ inch; for a smaller size, subtract $\frac{1}{2}$ inch.

To help you, alternative stitch directions have been given in brackets in the text.

The adjustment in length of skirts and dresses and coats without pockets should be made below the hip. Coats with inserted pockets, before the insertion of pockets.

The length of jumpers, dress bodices and sleeves should be adjusted before armhole is reached.

Finishing off a garment

Before any attempt is made to join the finished pieces of a garment, see that all loose ends are neatly darned in on the wrong side of work. Press each piece separately—and here I must say that this is where you can either make or mar a garment, so do not overpress. With the wrong side of the fabric facing, smooth the pieces out on to a padded surface and place pins all round the edges. Measure up and down and also across to ensure you have the correct size, taking care to keep rows and/or patterns straight. Lay a damp cloth over the work and press very gently using a moderately hot iron. A very light hand is most essential when pressing crepe wool, as overpressing will spoil the appearance of this beautifully finished fabric. Openwork patterns also need very light pressing—if these are overpressed, all the character will be taken out of the work.

Joining seams: this, in my opinion, depends on the pattern and texture of wool used in the garment. If the pattern is a fairly open one and the wool a fine ply, a dc. seam gives a neat finish. If the original wool is of a coarse texture, use a matching wool in a finer ply.

Alternatively with a close stitch design, sew the seams together. A good and simple method is to lay the two pieces to be sewn side by side with right side of work facing and draw the loop of each stitch on either side together, being careful to match patterns or/and rows. Turn work over and catch the remaining loops on the wrong side. The sewing must be done fairly loosely—but not too loosely—to allow for the stretching of the garment.

Press all seams after joining. Dc. borders must be sewn together in the same method as given for sewing seams.

How to learn crochet

Fig 1 How to make a Slip loop.

Start, by making a slip loop with the wool as in fig 1. Then:
1. Hold loop in place between thumb and forefinger of left hand.
With right hand, take hold of broad bar of hook as you would
a pencil. Insert your hook through loop with right hand.

2. Now pull short end of wool and ball in opposite directions to
bring loop close around the end of the hook, but not too tightly.

3. Hold the hook with the loop on, between the thumb and
forefinger of the left hand, pass wool over the first 3 fingers and
under and then over the little finger of the left hand. Now gently
pull wool so that it lies over and around your fingers firmly but
not tightly. Transfer hook into your right hand, holding knot of
loop between the thumb and forefinger of the left hand. Take
hold of the broad bar of hook in right hand as you would a
pencil and bring middle finger forward to rest near tip of hook.

The stitches

Chain stitch (ch.) This is the foundation of all crochet. Adjust fingers of left hand as in fig 2.

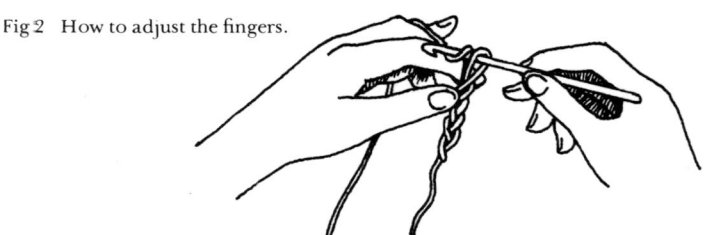

Fig 2   How to adjust the fingers.

The middle finger is raised to regulate the tension whilst the 3rd and little fingers prevent the wool from running too freely. The motion of the hook in the right hand and the wool in the left hand should be smooth-running. This will come with practice. Now with hands and wool in position, pass your hook under and catch wool with hook (fig 3) draw through loop on hook (fig 4).

Fig 3   Chain Stitch (Ch. st.)   Fig 4   Chain Stitch (Ch. st.)

Repeat this step until you have the required number of ch. st. Keep the thumb and forefinger of your left hand near the st. on which you are working.

The suppleness of the wrists plays a part in crochet. Two of the faults that newcomers to crochet make are to work either too tightly or too loosely. Don't let this worry you. Try to relax your

hands and wrists. Ease, together with an even tension, will come
with practice. Work a practice ch. until you have an even tension.

Fig 5   Slip Stitch (Sl. st.)

Slip stitch (sl. st) This is used when an invisible st. is required.
Good examples of this are the armholes and the shaping of the
shoulders.

Insert hook into the 2 top loops of st. W.o.h. and with one
motion draw through st. and loop on hook. One loop remains
on hook.

N.B. It is usual in all crochet to pick up the 2 top loops of each
st. unless otherwise stated.

Double crochet (dc.) This st. makes a firm fabric which is attractive
for a suit and also effective for borders on jumpers and cardigans.
Make a ch. of 20 for a practice piece.

1st row
1. Insert hook from the front under the 2 top threads of 2nd ch.
from hook.
2. Catch wool with hook (fig 6) and draw through ch. There are
now 2 loops on hook (fig 7).
3. W.o.h. and draw through 2 loops, 1 loop remains on hook
(fig 8).

Fig 6   Double Crochet (dc.)

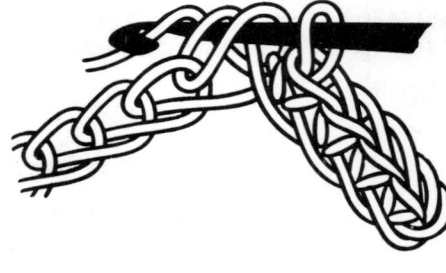

Fig 7   Double Crochet (dc.)

Fig 8   Double Crochet (dc.)

4. For next dc., insert hook under 2 threads of next ch. and repeat steps 2 and 3.

5. *Repeat* step 4 until you have a dc. in each st. At the end of the row, work 2 ch. to turn. This enables you to turn your work easily. Now turn your work with the reverse side facing you.

2nd row

1. Insert hook under 2 top loops of the first st. (The last loop made on the previous row.)

2. W.o.h. and draw through st., 2 loops on hook.

3. W.o.h. and draw through 2 loops, 1 loop on hook.

4. For next dc. insert hook under the 2 top loops of next st. and *repeat* steps 2 and 3.

Repeat step 4 until you have worked a dc. into every st., 2 ch. Turn. The 2 turning ch. of each row is *not* counted as a st. in the following row. *Repeat* this row until you have become familiar with the st. Fasten off.

How to fasten off
Omit the turning ch. at the end of last row, cut wool a few inches from work, bring loose end through the loop on hook and pull tightly.

Fig 9   Half Treble (Hlf. tr.)

Half Treble (hlf. tr.) makes an attractive firm fabric, and is a favourite of mine for children's clothes.
Commence with 20 ch. for a practice piece.

1st row
1. W.o.h. (fig 9) insert hook from the front under 2 top loops of 3rd ch. from hook.
2. W.o.h. and pull loop through ch., 3 loops on hook, w.o.h. (fig 10) draw through all loops on hook, 1 loop remains on hook (fig 11). A hlf. tr. is now completed.
3. For next half. tr., w.o.h. Insert hook under the 2 top threads of next ch.
4. *Repeat* steps 2 and 3 until 1 hlf. tr. has been made in each ch. At the end of the row make 2 ch. Turn.

2nd row
1. W.o.h. Insert hook under the 2 top loops of 1st st., i.e. the last st. on previous row.

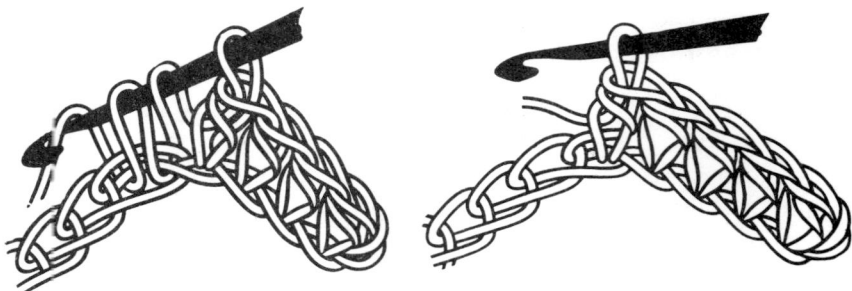

Fig 10 Half Treble (Hlf. tr.)   Fig 11 Half Treble (Hlf. tr.)

2. W.o.h. and pull through st. There are now 3 loops on hook, w.o h. and draw through all loops on hook.

3. For next hlf. tr., w.o.h., insert hook under the 2 top loops of next st. and *repeat* step 2.

4. *Repeat* steps 3 and 2 until 1 hlf. tr. has been made in each st., 2 ch. Turn.

N.B. The 2 ch. turning st. of each row does not count as a st. on the following rows.

Treble (tr.) is the most popular st. in crochet because so many different designs can be made from it.

Commence with a practice piece of 20 ch.

1st row

1. W.o.h. (fig 12) insert hook under the 2 top threads of the 4th ch. from hook.

2. W.o.h. and draw through st. There are now 3 loops on hook (fig 13).

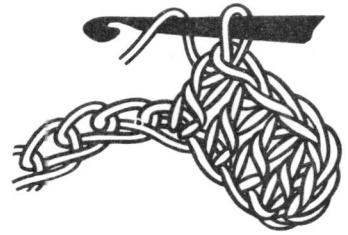

Fig 12 Treble (Tr.)

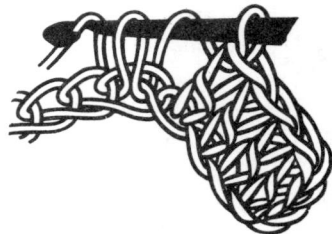

Fig 13 Treble (Tr.)

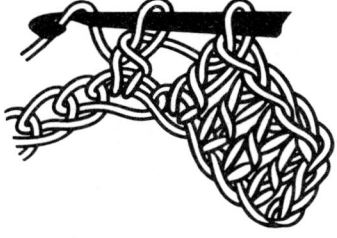

Fig 14 Treble (Tr.)

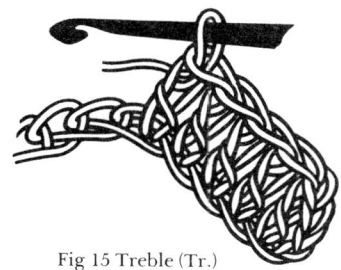

Fig 15 Treble (Tr.)

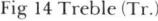

3. W.o.h. and draw through 2 loops, 2 loops remain on hook (fig 14).

4. W.o.h. again and draw through 2 remaining sts. 1 loop remains on hook (fig 15) 1 tr. is now completed.

5. For next tr. w.o.h., insert hook under 2 top threads of next ch. and *repeat* steps 2–5 until 1 tr. has been made in each ch.

6. At the end of the row, work 3 ch. Turn.

N.B. Turning ch. here counts as the 1st tr. on next and every following row, therefore the 1st tr. of each row is always missed.

2nd row

1. W.o.h. insert hook under the 2 top loops of the 5th st. from the hook (the 2nd tr. of previous row).

Repeat steps 2–6 of 1st row working last tr. into top of 3 turning ch.

Repeat the 2nd row until you are familiar with st. Fasten off.

Double treble (dbl. tr.) This is a st. which is rarely used by itself, though one can make most attractive designs combining it with other basic sts.

Make a practice ch. of 20.

1st row

1. W.o.h. 2 times and insert hook under the 2 top threads of the 5th ch. from hook.

2. W.o.h. and draw through the ch. There are now 4 loops on the hook (fig 16).

3. W.o.h. again and draw through 2 loops (3 loops remain on hook).

Fig 16 Double Treble (Dbl. tr.)

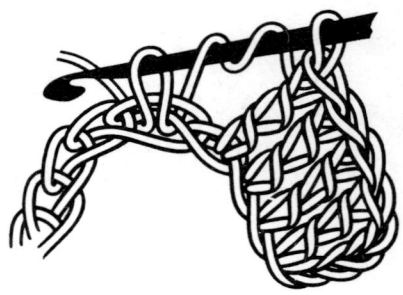

4. W.o.h. and draw through 2 loops (2 loops remain on hook).
5. W.o.h. once again and draw through the remaining 2 loops (1 loop remains on hook).
6. For the next dbl. tr. W.o.h., 2 times and insert hook under the 2 top threads of next ch. *Repeat* steps 2–6 until 1 dbl. tr. has been made in each ch.
7. At the end of the row make 4 ch. and turn. The turning 4 ch. counts as the first dbl. tr. on the next row and every following row. therefore the first dbl. tr. is always missed.

2nd row
1. Insert hook under the 2 top loops of the 6th st. from hook (2nd st. on previous row).
2. *Repeat* steps 2–7 on 1st row working last dbl. tr. into top of 4 turning ch.
Repeat 2nd row until you are familiar with this st. Fasten off.

Turning at ends of rows
A certain number of ch. are worked at the end of each row to bring work into position for the next row. The number of turning ch. required is always dependent on the st. that you intend to begin the next row with.
Dc.
2 ch. to turn.
Hlf. tr.
2 ch. to turn.
Tr.
3 ch. to turn.
Dbl. tr.
4 ch. to turn.

How to decrease in crochet
Dc.
Work off 2 dc. thus: Insert hook into next dc. and pull loop
through. Insert hook into the following dc.—pull loop through
(3 loops on hook). W.o.h. and draw through all loops on hook.
Hlf. tr.
Work off 2 half. tr. as 1 hlf. tr. thus: * W.o.h. draw a loop
through next hlf. tr. *Repeat* from * once more (5 loops on hook)
w.o.h. and draw through all loops on hook.
Tr.
Work off 2 tr. as 1 tr. thus: * W.o.h. draw a loop through next
tr. (3 loops on hook) w.o.h. and draw through 2 loops (2 loops
on hook). *

Repeat from * once more (3 loops on hook) w.o.h. and draw
through all loops on hook.

Inc.
By working 2 sts. into 1 st.

Tension or gauge
This means the number of st. per inch and the number of rows
per inch. The tension is most important but it is something which
can always be adjusted, quite easily. Before starting a garment
always work a 3-inch sample square of the pattern. Pin this down
on to a cloth and mark off with pins a 2-inch measurement in
the centre of the square and see if the tension corresponds with
the directions in the pattern. If you have more rows and sts., use
a larger-size hook. Should you have fewer rows and sts. use a
smaller-size hook. An even tension should be achieved if you
hold your work firmly in the left hand with the wool running
freely. Try to keep the right hand and wrist relaxed and supple.
Do not be discouraged if you do not achieve an even tension at
first. This will come with practice. However do *not* begin your
garment until your tension corresponds with the directions in the
pattern.

Wools and hook
Crochet gives a firm fabric in any type of wool and never before
has there been such a variety available, both in type and colour.

For an easy-to-work wool suitable for a beginner, a wool with a
firm twist is excellent. This if used with a smooth hook with a
narrow rounded end enables beginners to crochet without any
difficulties.

Joining of wool

Knots must never be used. If 3 or 4 ply wool is being used, thread
the new ball of wool into a darning needle and weave it through
the end of the wool just used for about 3 inches. Smooth it out
between thumb and finger and cut off loose ends of wool. If
thicker wool is being used, either join at the end of a row or
unravel the ends for about 4–5 inches, cut away 1 strand from
each end of the wool and twist the remaining strands together.
Cut away loose ends.

Measuring

Work must always be measured on the straight of a garment. The
depth of the armhole is measured on the straight from the 1st row
of the dec. Do not rely altogether on the tape measure or ruler.
With crochet one must also count. It has been said 'If you can
count, you can crochet', so do remember to count the rows or
patterns on pieces that are to be joined together and work exactly
the same number on each one, e.g. the Back and the Front of a
skirt.

Casting-off in crochet

Break off the wool, leaving sufficient over to weave in, then draw
the end of the wool through the loop, pulling tightly.

Pressing

This must be done with great care. You can spoil a garment by
over-pressing. Each piece should be pressed separately before
sewing-up, so with the wrong side of the fabric facing, smooth out
on to a padded surface and place pins all around the edges.
Measure up, down and across to ensure that you have the correct
size, taking care to keep the rows or patterns straight. I like to
use a steam iron for pressing crochet garments. Just skim over the
surface of the fabric without actually touching it. However if a
steam iron is not available use a damp cloth, a fairly hot iron and,
most essential of all, a light hand. This is particularly true if crepe

has been used as over-pressing spoils the appearance of this beautifully finished fabric. Do not remove the pins from the blocked pieces until the pieces are fully dry.

Man-made yarns such as Nylon, Courtelle etc.
The manufacturers of these yarns stipulate that pressing is not necessary, but my own personal views are that a very light pressing will enhance the appearance of the finished garment.

Making-up a garment
This, in my opinion, depends on the pattern used in the garment. With most patterns, however, I prefer to crochet the seams together with a dc. st. as this gives a much neater finish. Alternatively sew the sides together with a fine back st., as close to the edge as possible. Whichever method is used, pin the seams together, making sure that rows or patterns match exactly. If the dc. method is being used and the original wool is of a coarse texture, use a matching one in a finer ply. If the original wool is a crepe and the sewing method is being used, this can be easily split into separate strands and used, thus resulting in an excellent fine seam. When joining the shoulder seams, take the line of stitching straight across the shapings. Press each seam as it is joined. Dc. borders must be sewn together using a flat seam.

Sleeveless cotton blouse

MATERIALS

7 (7–8) balls Twilley's Lyscordet or the same quantity of Strutt's
Knitting Cotton No. 5. Crochet hook size 2.50 (U.S. C).

Measurements

To fit 34 (36–38) ins. bust. Length from shoulder 19 ins.

Tension

6 groups = 3 ins. 5 rows = 1½ ins.

METHOD

Back

Make 97 (103–109) chain.

1st row:

2 tr. into 4th ch. from hook, * miss 2 ch., 3 tr. into next ch.
Repeat from * to end, 4 ch., turn. (32 (34–36) grps. of trs.)

2nd row:

3 tr. into space between first 2 grps., * 3 tr. into next space
between grps. Repeat from * ending with 1 ch., 1 tr. into turning
ch. 3 ch., turn.

3rd row:

2 tr. into 1 ch. space preceding first grp., * 3 tr. into each space
to end., 4 ch., turn.

Repeat 2nd and 3rd rows alternately until work measures 12 ins.
or length desired to armhole, ending with 3rd row.

Armhole shaping

Sl. st. over 2 (2–3) grps. and into first tr. of next grp., 4 ch., *

3 tr. into next space. Repeat from * until 3 (3–4) grps. remain, 1 ch., 1 tr. into 3rd tr. of next grp., 3 ch., turn (2 (2–3) grps. remain unworked.)

Work straight in pattern for 20 (20–22) rows. (28 (30–30) grps.)

Shaping shoulder

Sl. st. over 3 grps., into next space work 1 dc., 1 hlf. tr., and 1 tr., work to last 4 grps., into next space work 1 tr., 1 hlf. tr. and 1 cc., sl. st. into next st. Turn.

Next row:

Sl. st. over 3 grps., 1 dc., 1 hlf. tr. and 1 tr. into next space, work to last 4 grps., 1 tr., 1 hlf. tr. and 1 dc. into next space, 1 sl. st. into next st. Turn.

Next row:

Sl. st. over 2 grps., 1 dc., 1 hlf. tr., 1 tr. into next space, work to last 3 grps., 1 tr., 1 hlf. tr. 1 dc. into next space, sl. st. into next st. Fasten off. (12 (14–14) grps. remain at back.)

Front

Work as for back until work measures 9 rows less than back.

Neck shaping

Work along 7 (8–8) grps., 4 ch., turn.
Work a further 8 rows straight to shoulder shaping.

Shoulder shaping: Neck edge

Work to last 4 grps., 1 tr., 1 hlf. tr. and 1 dc. into next space, sl. st. into next st., turn.

Next row:

Sl. st. over 2 (3–3) grps., 1 dc., 1 hlf. tr., 1 tr. into next space, work in pattern to end. Fasten off.

Second side of front

Miss 14 grps. on front and rejoin cotton into top of 3rd tr. of next grp. and work as opposite side reversing shoulder shaping. Fasten off.

Making up

Press pieces separately under a damp cloth using a fairly hot iron. With right side facing, join seams together thus: lay the two pieces to be sewn side by side and carefully draw the loop of each stitch together, matching rows.

Borders

Lower edge

With right side facing, rejoin cotton to side seam. Work 3 dc. into each space all round, 2 ch., turn.

Next row:

1 dc. into each dc. to end, 2 ch., turn. Repeat this row once more, omitting turning ch.

Next row:

With wrong side of work facing, 1 sl. st. into each dc. taking care not to work too tightly. Fasten off.

Armholes

With right side facing, rejoin cotton at armhole and work 2 dc. into each tr. row end, join with sl. st., 2 ch., turn.

Next row:

1 dc. into each st. decreasing 1 dc. at each side of shoulder seam, 2 ch., turn. Repeat this row once more omitting turning ch.

Next row:

With wrong side of work facing, 1 sl. st. into each dc. Fasten off.

Neck edge

With right side facing, rejoin cotton at back of neck and work 1 dc. into each tr. along back, 2 dc. into each tr. row end along shoulder, 1 dc. into each tr. along front and 2 dc. into each tr. row end along second shoulder, join with sl. st. into corner, 2 ch., turn.

Next row:

Dec. 1 dc., 1 dc. into each st. to within last 2 dc. at corner of shoulder, dec. 1 dc., 1 dc. into corner st., dec. 1 dc., 1 dc. into each st. along front to last 2 dc. before corner; dec. 1 dc., 1 dc. into corner st., dec. 1 dc., 1 dc. into each st. along second shoulder to corner; dec. 1 dc., 1 dc. into corner st., dec. 1 dc., 1 dc. into each st. along back to corner; dec. 1 dc., 1 dc. into corner st. Join with sl. st. into turning ch., 2 ch., turn. Mark all corner sts. with contrast cotton.

Work a further 3 rows dc. decreasing at each side of corner st. on every row. Turn.

Next row:

(Wrong side of work facing)

1 sl. st. into each dc. Fasten off.

Darn all loose ends in neatly on wrong side. Press borders and seams.

Nightdress yoke

MATERIALS

Twilley's Lyscordet—2 balls Citrus Green; 2 (3) 3 balls Black: or any two colours of choice. Crochet hook size 2.50 (U.S. C).

Measurements

To fit 33–34 (35–36) 37–38 inch bust.

METHOD

Back

Using Black, make 115 (125) 135 chain.

1st row:

Leaving the last loop of each on hook, 2 dbl. tr. into 5th ch. from hook, w.o.h. and draw through all 3 loops on hook, 4 ch., leaving the last loop of each on hook, 3 dbl. tr. into same ch. as last dbl. tr., w.o.h. and draw through all loops on hook, miss 4 ch., * leaving the last loop of each on hook 3 dbl. tr. into next ch., w.o.h. and draw through all 4 loops on hook, 4 ch., leaving the last loop of each on hook, 3 dbl. tr. into same ch., w.o.h. and draw through all loops on hook. (These 3 dbl. trs., 4 ch. and 3 dbl. trs. form one grp.) Miss 4 ch. Repeat from * ending with 1 grp. into last ch. (23 (25) 27 grps.)

2nd row:

4 ch. (counts as first dbl. tr. of $\frac{1}{2}$ grp.) and 2 dbl. tr. into top of first $\frac{1}{2}$ grp., w.o.h. and draw through 3 loops on hook, * miss 4 ch. ($\frac{1}{2}$ grp., 4 ch. and $\frac{1}{2}$ grp.) into top of next $\frac{1}{2}$ grp. (This gives a complete grp. between the grps. of previous row.) Repeat from * ending with miss 4 ch., $\frac{1}{2}$ grp. into top of last $\frac{1}{2}$ grp. Break off black cotton.

3rd row:

Join in Citrus Green. 2 ch., 2 dc. into top of grp., 3 dc. over 4

ch. space, * 2 dc. into top of next grp., 3 dc. over next 4 ch.
space. Repeat from * ending with 2 dc. into top of last grp., 2
ch., turn.

4th row:
1 dc. into each dc. to end. Break off Citrus Green cotton.

5th row:
Miss 16 dc. Join in Black cotton. 4 ch. ($\frac{1}{2}$ grp., 4 ch. and $\frac{1}{2}$ grp.)
into first dc., * miss 4 dc. ($\frac{1}{2}$ grp., 4 ch. and $\frac{1}{2}$ grp.) into next dc.
Repeat from * to within last 3 grps., 4 ch., turn. (17 (19) 21 grps.)

6th row:
As 2nd row. Break off Black cotton.

7th row:
Join in Citrus Green. Work as 3rd row.

8th row:
As 4th row. Break off Citrus Green cotton.
Continue straight in pattern (changing the colours in cotton as
before) until 3 complete patterns and 3 rows of 4th pattern have
been worked. Fasten off.

Front

Work as for back until 2 complete patterns and 3 rows of 3rd
pattern have been worked, 2 ch., turn.

Next row:
1 dc. into each of next 22 dc., 4 ch., turn.
Work straight in pattern on these 5 grps. for 7 (8) 8 complete
patterns and 3 rows of next pattern. Fasten off.
Work opposite shoulder to correspond.

Join shoulders to back of yoke

With right side facing, lay the two edges to be sewn side by side
and draw the loops of each side together carefully taking up one
loop of each dc. Turn and work the same on the wrong side.

Neck edge

With right side facing, join in black cotton and work along each
shoulder at neck edge thus—4 dc. along each pattern row end and
2 dc. over the dc. row ends (10 dc. over one complete pattern).
Fasten off.

Next row:
Join in Citrus Green and with right side of work facing, work 1

dc. into each dc. all round, decreasing 1 dc. at each corner of back and front. Join with sl. st.

Next row:

Still with right side facing, work picot edging as follows—* 3 ch., 1 dc. into 3rd ch. from hook, miss 2 dc., sl. st. into next dc. Repeat from * all round, join with sl. st. Fasten off. Sew side seams.

Armholes

Using Black cotton, work 1 row dc. (4 dc. over pattern row ends and 2 dc. over dc. row ends). Fasten off.

Next row:

Join in Citrus Green and with right side facing work 1 dc. into each dc. all round. Turn and work 1 sl. st. into each dc. taking care not to work the sl. st. too tightly.

Lower edge of yoke

Join in Black cotton and work 3 dc. over each 4 ch. space and 2 dc. into each grp. all round. Fasten off.

Next row:

Join in Citrus Green and with right side facing work 1 dc. into each dc. all round, 2 ch., turn.

Next row:

1 dc. into each dc. all round. Fasten off.

Next row:

Join in Black and with right side facing work picot edge as for neck. Fasten off.

Darn all ends in neatly on wrong side of work and press lightly also on wrong side.

Tabard

MATERIALS

The original was made in Paton's Totem Double Crepe Wool—4 ozs. or 2 50-gr. balls in Beau Blue; 5 ozs. or 3 50-gr. balls in Wild Rose; 6 ozs. or 3 50-gr. balls in Hot Pink (this includes fringe); 2 ozs. or 1 50-gr. ball in Marine Blue; or any colour scheme to your own choice. If this is not available, any double crepe wool or synthetic yarn may be used. Crochet hook size 3.50 (U.S. E). 4 buttons.

Length without fringe

25 ins.

Measurements

To fit 34–35 ins. bust. To make 36–37 ins. bust, use crochet hook size 4.00 (U.S. F).
Twisted treble = tw. tr. W.o.h., insert hook into stitch, w.o.h. and draw through loop and 'over' in one motion (2 loops on hook), w.o.h. and draw through 2 loops on hook.

METHOD

Back

Working from left side and beginning with Beau blue wool, make 72 chain.

1st row:

Tw. tr. into 3rd ch. from hook, tw. tr. into each ch. to end, 2 ch., turn. (70 tw. tr.)

2nd and 3rd rows:

Tw. tr. into each st. to end, 2 ch., turn.

Begin shaping armholes
4th row:
Tw. tr. into first st., 2 tw. tr. into next st. (increase made) 1 tw.
tr. into each st. to end, 2 ch., turn. (71 tw. tr.)
5th row:
Tw. tr. until 2 sts. remain, increase in next st., 1 tw. tr. into last
st., 2 ch., turn.
6th row:
As 4th row.

7th row:
As 5th row, omitting the 2 ch. turn (74 tw. tr.). Make 35 chain, turn.

8th row:
Tw. tr. into 3rd ch. from hook, tw. tr. into each ch., tw. tr. into each st. to end, 2 ch., turn. (107 tw. tr.)

Begin shaping shoulder
9th row:
Tw. tr. to last 2 sts., increase in next st., 1 tw. tr. into end st., 1 ch., turn.

10th row:
1 dc. into each st. to end. Break off blue wool.

11th row:
Join in Marine blue wool. 1 dc. into first dc. * 1 tr. into st. below next dc., 1 dc. into next dc. Repeat from * to end, 1 ch., turn.

12th row:
1 dc. into each st. to end. Break off Marine blue wool.

13th row:
Join in Wild Rose wool. Repeat 11th row, 2 ch., turn.

14th row:
Tw. tr. into first st., inc. in next st., tw. tr. to end, 2 ch., turn. (109 tw. tr.)

15th row:
Tw. tr. into each st., 2 ch., turn.
Repeat the last 2 rows alternately 3 times more, 1 ch., turn. (112 tw. tr.)

22nd row:
1 dc. into each st. Break off Wild Rose wool.

23rd row:
Join in Hot Pink wool. Repeat 11th row, 2 ch., turn. Work straight in tw. tr. for 10 rows, 1 ch., turn.

34th row:
1 dc. into each st. Break off Hot Pink wool.

35th row:
Join in Marine blue wool. Repeat 11th row, 2 ch., turn. Work 2 rows straight in tw. tr., 1 ch., turn.

38th row:
1 dc. into each st. Break off Marine blue wool.

39th row:
Join in Hot Pink wool. Repeat 11th row, 2 ch., turn. Work
straight in tw. tr. for 10 rows, 1 ch., turn.
50th row:
1 dc. into each st. Break off Hot pink wool.
51st row:
Join in Wild Rose wool. Repeat 11th row, 2 ch., turn.
52nd row:
Tw. tr. into first st., decrease 1 tw. tr., tw. tr. to end, 2 ch., turn.
53rd row:
Tw. tr. into each st., 2 ch., turn. Repeat the last two rows 3 times
more, 1 ch., turn. (108 tw. tr.)
60th row:
1 dc. into each st. Break off Wild Rose wool.
61st row:
Join in Marine Blue wool. Repeat 11th row.
62nd row:
1 dc. into each st. Break off Marine Blue wool.
63rd row:
Join in Beau Blue wool: Repeat 11th row, 2 ch., turn.
64th row:
Tw. tr. into first st., dec. 1 st., tw. tr. to end, 2 ch., turn.
65th row:
Tw. tr. into each st. Break off wool.

Armhole
66th row:
Miss 33 tw. tr. Rejoin blue wool into next st. and work in tw. tr.
to end, 2 ch., turn.
67th row:
Tw. tr. to last 3 sts., dec. 1 st., 1 tw. tr. into last st., 2 ch., turn.
68th row:
Tw. tr. into first st., dec. 1 st., tw. tr. to end., 2 ch., turn.
69th row:
As 67th row. (70 tw. tr.)
Work 2 rows straight in tw. tr., 1 ch., turn.
Next row:
1 dc. into each st. Fasten off.

Front

Make 72 chain with Beau Blue wool and work as for back from rows 1 to 22 inclusive.

23rd row:

Join in Hot Pink wool. Repeat 11th row of back until 7 sts. remain, 2 ch., turn.

Shaping neck

Work 10 rows in tw. tr. decreasing 1 st. at neck edge on every row. 1 ch., turn. (95 tw. tr.)

34th row:

1 dc. into each st. Break off Hot Pink wool.

35th row:

Join in Marine Blue wool. Repeat 11th row of back, 2 ch., turn. Work 2 rows straight in tw. tr., 1 ch., turn.

38th row:

1 dc. into each st. Break off Marine Blue wool.

39th row:

Join in Hot Pink wool. Repeat 11th row of back, 2 ch., turn. Work 10 rows in tw. tr. increasing 1 st. at neck edge on every row, 1 ch., turn. (105 tw. tr.)

50th row:

1 dc. into each st. Break off Hot Pink wool.

51st row:

Join in Wild Rose wool. Repeat 11th row of back, 9 ch., turn.

52nd row:

1 tw. tr. into 3rd ch. from hook, 1 tw. tr. into each of next 6 ch., tw. tr. to end, 2 ch., turn. (112 tw. tr.)

Shaping shoulder

53rd row:

Work 7 rows in tw. tr. decreasing at shoulder on the first and each alternate row 4 times, 1 ch., turn. (108 tw. tr.)

60th row:

1 dc. into each st. Break off Wild Rose wool.

Work as for back from 61st row to end inclusive. Fasten off. Darn all ends in neatly on wrong side.

Press each piece separately and join shoulder seams thus: with right sides facing, lay the two edges to be sewn side by side and carefully draw the loops of each together, using wool that matches. Press seams.

With right side facing and with Beau Blue wool, work 1 row dc. round each armhole.

Neck edge
1st row:
With Hot Pink wool work 76 dc. evenly all round, 1 ch., turn.
2nd row:
1 dc. into each st. join with sl. st. Fasten off.
With Beau Blue wool, join side seams from armhole to waistline—approx. 5½ ins. in the same way as shoulder seams.

Tabs
With Hot Pink wool make 12 chain and work 4 rows in tw. tr. (10 tw. tr.)
1st buttonhole row:
Work 3 tw. tr., 4 ch., miss 4 sts., 1 tw. tr. into each of next 3 tw. tr., 2 ch., turn.
2nd buttonhole row:
3 tw. tr., 4 tw. tr. into 4 ch. space, 3 tw. tr., 2 ch., turn. Work straight until work measures 7 ins. Do not break off wool but continue down first long side edge working a row dc. down this edge and along short end, up the other side edge and along top end. Join with sl. st. Fasten off. With Beau Blue wool work 2 rows dc. around side slits. Fasten off.

Sew a button on each side of front approx. 4 ins from lower edge of tabard and 1½ ins from side edge. Button on tabs and attach other end of tabs to back of tabard and secure with button.

Fringe
Optional.
Approx. 4 ins in length. Cut Hot Pink wool into 8-inch lengths and knot into lower edge of garment.

Skirt in crochet ribbing

MATERIALS
17 ozs. Paton's Cameo Crepe Wool. Crochet hook size 3.00 (U.S. D). 1-inch wide elastic, waist size. If the specified wool is not available, substitute a fine 4-ply crepe or synthetic yarn.

Measurements
To fit 38-inch hip. Length 24 ins. or length desired.

Tension
7 raised trs. = 1 inch; 6 rows = 1 inch.

This skirt can be made in any size. See 'Adjusting patterns for different measurements' (page 11). It can also have coloured stripes round lower edge to suit individual tastes.
This garment is worked in 'raised' and 'depressed' trebles as follows:

To make a 'raised' treble
W.o.h. as for a tr., insert hook from the front between the 'bars' of 2 trs., pass hook round back of tr. and out through next space to front of work and finish the tr. in the usual way.

To make a 'depressed' treble
W.o.h., insert hook from the back between the 'bars' of 2 trs., pass hook in front of 1 tr. and through next space to back of work and finish tr. in the usual way.

METHOD
Beginning at waist. Make 274 chain. Work in rounds.
1st round:
1 tr. into 4th ch. from hook, 1 tr. into each ch. to end. Join with sl. st. into top of 3 starting ch. There should be 271 tr. not counting the 3 turning ch.

2nd round:
3 ch., miss first tr., 1 'raised' tr. round next tr., * 1 'depressed' tr. round next tr., 1 'raised' tr. round next tr. Repeat from * all round ending with a 'raised' tr., sl. st. into top of 3 turning ch.

N.B.
Be careful to work the sl. st. into the *top* of 3 turning ch. or the work may twist as this forms the 'depressed' tr. between the first and last 'raised' trs.

Repeat this round until work measures 1 inch, keeping 'raised' trs. over 'raised' trs. and 'depressed' trs. over 'depressed' trs.

Next round:
Work in ribbing of 8 'raised' trs. and 1 'depressed' tr. as follows: 3 ch., * 1 raised tr., 1 tr. between trs. (increase) 1 raised tr. round each of next 6 tr., depressed tr. round next tr. (raised tr. round each of next 8 tr., depressed tr. round next tr.) 3 times. Repeat from * 7 times more, omitting the depressed tr. at end of round, join with sl. st. to top of 3 ch. (8 trs. increased). 32 groups of ribbing.

Work straight in rounds keeping raised trs. over raised trs. and
depressed trs. over depressed trs. for length desired. Fasten off.
Press lightly on wrong side under damp cloth and then *very lightly*
on right side.

Waistline
Cut elastic to waist measurement and join into circle. Sew to
waist-band distributing fullness evenly and using herringbone
stitch, catching elastic above and below as you work to prevent
elastic rolling.

Crochet suit with raglan sleeves and mitred borders

MATERIALS

The original was made with 27 balls of Jaeger's Courtelle 4-ply. If this is not available, any synthetic yarn may be used. Approx. quantity—32 20-gr. balls or 16 40-gr. balls. Crochet hooks Nos 2.50 and 2.00 (U.S. C and B). 6 small button moulds. 1-inch wide elastic for waistband.

Measurements

To fit 36-38 inch bust. Length of coat 22 ins. Length of sleeve 13 ins. Length of skirt 25 ins.

Tension

5 grps = 3 ins. 12 rows (3 patterns) = $3\frac{1}{4}$ ins. approx.

N.B. For the larger figure: 40–41 bust size, use crochet hooks sizes 3.00 and 2.50 (U.S. D and C).

Tension

5 grps. = $3\frac{1}{2}$ ins. 12 rows (3 patterns) = $3\frac{1}{2}$ ins.

Measurements

Length of coat 24 ins. Length of sleeve seam $14\frac{3}{4}$ ins.

Materials

29 Balls Jaeger Courtelle 4-ply.

METHOD
COAT

Make 149 chain.

Back

1st row:

Leaving the last loop of each on hook, 2 tr. into 4th ch. from
hook, w.o.h. and draw through all 3 loops on hook, 3 ch., leaving
the last loop of each on hook, 3 tr. into the same ch. as last grp.,
w.o.h. and draw through all 4 loops on hook, miss 4 ch., * leaving
the last loop of each on hook, 3 tr. into next ch., w.o.h. and draw
through all loops on hook, 3 ch., leaving the last loop of each
on hook, 3 tr. into same ch., w.o.h. and draw through all loops
on hook. (These 3 tr., 3 ch., 3 tr. form 1 grp.) Miss 4 ch. Repeat
from * to last ch., 1 grp. into last ch. (30 grps.)

2nd row:

3 ch. (this forms the first tr. of $\frac{1}{2}$ grp.), 2 tr. into top of first $\frac{1}{2}$ grp., w.o.h. and draw through 3 loops on hook, * miss 3 ch. ($\frac{1}{2}$ grp., 3 ch., $\frac{1}{2}$ grp. into top of next $\frac{1}{2}$ grp.). (This gives a complete grp. between the grps. of previous row). Repeat from * ending with miss 3 ch., $\frac{1}{2}$ grp. into top of last $\frac{1}{2}$ grp.

3rd row:

2 ch., 2 dc. into top of grp., 3 dc. over 3 ch. space, * 1 dc. into top of next grp., 3 dc. over 3 ch. space. Repeat from * 1 dc. into top of last grp., turn.

4th row:

2 ch., 1 dc. into each dc. to end, turn.

5th row:

3 ch., 2 tr. into 2nd dc., ($\frac{1}{2}$ grp.), 3 ch., $\frac{1}{2}$ grp. into same dc., * miss 3 dc., ($\frac{1}{2}$ grp., 3 ch., $\frac{1}{2}$ grp. into next dc.). Repeat from * to end, turn.

6th row:

As 2nd row.

7th row:

As 3rd row.

8th row:

As 4th row.

Rows 5–8 inclusive form the pattern.

Work straight until 8 complete patterns have been worked. With right side facing, shape raglan armhole by omitting $\frac{1}{2}$ grp. at beginning and end of each row until 7 complete grps. and $\frac{1}{2}$ grp. at each end remain. Fasten off.

11 complete patterns in raglan shaping.

Left front

Make 74 chain. (15 grps.)

Work as given for back to beginning of raglan shaping. With right side facing, shape raglan as given for back by decreasing $\frac{1}{2}$ grp. as before at beginning of row and then on every row at this edge until 5 grps. and $\frac{1}{2}$ grp. at each end remain. (Eight complete patterns and 2 rows of 9th have been worked from beginning of raglan shaping.)

Next row:

Work in dc. to within last $1\frac{1}{2}$ grps., turn.

Next row:
2 ch., dc. to end.
Continue raglan shaping and at the same time omitting $\frac{1}{2}$ grp. on each row at neck edge on the following 2 complete patterns (two $\frac{1}{2}$ grps. remain). Fasten off.

Right front
15 grps. Work as for left front reversing raglan and neck shapings.

Sleeves
Make 84 chain. (17 grps.)
Work in pattern until 10 complete patterns have been worked, increasing 1 grp. at each end of the first row of 3rd, 5th, 7th and 9th pattern. (25 grps.) Work raglan shaping as given for back until 2 grps. and $\frac{1}{2}$ grp. at each end remain. 11 complete patterns in raglan shaping. Fasten off. Press each piece carefully on wrong side. Join raglan seams, matching the patterns, using the dc. method.

Borders: Lower edge of back
With right side facing, work 2 dc. into base of first grp., * 3 dc. into next 4 ch. loop, 1 dc. into base of next grp. Repeat from * to last grp., 2 dc. into base of last grp., 2 ch., turn. Work in dc. for a further 16 rows. Fasten off.

Fronts, revers and collar
Beginning at side seam at lower edge of right front and with right side facing, work 2 dc. into base of first grp., * 3 dc. into 4 ch. loop, 1 dc. into base of next grp. Repeat from * along lower edge to corner of right front, 1 dc. into corner (mark corner st. with contrast wool). Continue up right front to beginning of neck shaping thus: * (3 dc. along side of next $\frac{1}{2}$ grp.) twice, 1 dc. into each of dc. rows, making 8 dc. into each complete pattern. Repeat from * to neck shaping, 1 dc. into corner of neck shaping (mark with contrast wool as before). 106 dc. evenly all round neck to beginning of neck shaping on left front, 1 dc. into corner (mark as before). Work down left front to correspond with right front, 1 dc. into corner of left front (mark as before), and along lower edge of front to correspond with right front. 2 ch., turn.

Work 7 more rows dc. increasing 1 dc. each side of each corner st. on every row (move contrast wool into single dc. on each row to obtain a good mitre).

Next row:
Make evenly spaced buttonholes on right front (5 ch., miss 5 dc.) and on next row work 5 dc. over each 5 ch.

Work a further 7 rows dc. increasing as before at corners. Fasten off.

Cuffs
With right side facing, work along lower edge of each sleeve as for back, 1 dc. into base of each grp., and 3 dc. over each 4 ch. loop. Work 17 rows decreasing 1 dc. each end of 5th row and each 5th row following. Fasten off. Press borders carefully. Join side and sleeve seams using a dc. method. Press seams.

Crochet buttons
Make 3 ch. and join with a sl. st. to form a ring.
Work 6 dc. into ring and join with a sl. st.

Next round:
* w.o.h., insert hook into centre of ring and draw loop through (w.o.h. and draw through 2 loops) twice (tr.). Repeat from * 12 times or until front of button is well covered.

Next round:
1 dc. into each st. Insert button mould and draw together. Sew buttons on coat.

SKIRT (Back and front alike)
Make skirt 2 ins. wider than hip measurement. Add 1 inch to back and front. Work in pattern straight for 19 ins. and then using a size smaller hook, work straight for a further 5 ins. Fasten off. Turn work to lower edge and with right side facing, work a dc. border as for back of coat. Press carefully. Join seams using a dc. method.
Join elastic to waist measurement and sew to waist of skirt using a herringbone stitch, catching elastic above and below as you work to prevent elastic rolling.

Shirtwaister dress

MATERIALS

The original was made in Lister's Crepe 4-ply. If this is not
available, a fine 4-ply pure crepe wool or any synthetic yarn may
be used. Approx. quantity—20 (22–24) ozs. or 10 (11–12) 40-gr.
balls of synthetic yarn. Crochet hook size 3.00 (U.S. D). 10 small
button moulds.

Measurements

34 (36–38) inch bust size. 36 (38–40) hip. Sleeve 12 inches.

Tension

3 groups approx. = 1 inch. 4 rows = 1½ inches approx.

METHOD

Back

Make 134 (140–146) chain.

1st row:

1 tr. into 4th ch. from hook, * 1 ch., leaving the last loop of each
on hook, 1 tr. into same ch. as last tr., miss 1 ch., 2 tr. into next
ch. (4 loops on hook) w.o.h. and draw through all loops on hook.
Repeat from * to end, 3 ch., turn. (66 (69–72) grps.)

2nd row:

1 tr. into 2nd st. of first grp. picking up 2 loops. * 1 ch., leaving
the last loop of each on hook, 1 tr. into same st. as last tr., miss
ch. st., 2 tr. into next st. picking up 2 loops (4 loops on hook),
w.o.h. and draw through all loops on hook. Repeat from * to end
working last 2 tr. into turning ch., 3 ch., turn.

The 2nd row forms the pattern and is repeated throughout.
Repeat this row for 7 ins. in length.

Next row:
Work 21 (22–23) grps., * 1 ch., leaving the last loop of each on
hook, work 1 tr. into same grp., 1 tr. into next grp., 2 tr. into
next grp. (5 loops on hook), w.o.h. and draw through all loops
on hook; * (1 grp. decreased), work 22 (23–24) grps. Repeat from
* to *, then work 21 (22–23) grps. to end, 3 ch., turn.
Work straight for a further 7 ins.
Next row:
20 (21–22) grps., decrease 1 grp., 22 (23–24) grps., decrease 1 grp.,
20 (21–22) grps. to end, 3 ch., turn. (62 (65–68) grps.)
Work straight up to hip length—18 ins. or length desired.

Darts
Work 19 (20–21) grps., dec. 1 grp., 22 (23–24) grps., dec. 1 grp.,
19 (20–21) grps., to end, 3 ch., turn.
Work 2 rows straight.

Repeat last 3 rows 4 times more having 1 grp. less at each side
edge on each decrease row. Work straight to waistline 24 ins. or
length desired. (52 (55–58) grps.) Mark waistline with contrast
wool.
Work 4 rows straight.
Next row:
Work 16 (17–18) grps., increase 1 grp. into ch. st. between grps.,
work to last 16 (17–18) grps., increase 1 grp. into ch. st. between
grps., 16 (17–18) grps. to end, 3 ch., turn.
Work 4 rows straight.
Next row:
17 (18–19) grps., inc. 1 grp., work to last 17 (18–19) grps., inc.
1 grp., work to end, 3 ch., turn.
Work 4 rows straight.
Next row:
18 (19–20) grps., inc. 1 grp., work to last 18 (19–20) grps., inc.
1 grp., work to end, 3 ch., turn.
Work 3 rows straight.
Next row:
Work 19 (20–21) grps., inc. 1 grp., work to last 19 (20–21) grps.,
inc. 1 grp., pattern to end, 3 ch., turn.
Work 1 row straight. Adjust length here.

Armhole shaping
1st row:
Sl. st. over 2 (2–3) grps., pattern to last 2 (2–3) grps., 3 ch., turn.
2nd row:
Pattern to last 3 grps., dec. 1 grp., 1 grp., 3 ch., turn.
Repeat 2nd row 7 times more.

Work straight until armhole measures $7\frac{1}{2}$ ($7\frac{1}{2}$–8) ins. from beginning of armhole shaping.

Shoulder shaping
Sl. st. over 5 grps., work to last 5 grps. (To eliminate steps omit the starting ch.) Sl. st. into next ch. st., turn.

Repeat this row twice more. 18 (21–22) grps. at back of neck.
Fasten off.

Pockets (2)
Make 30 chain (14 grps.). Work in pattern for 10 rows. Fasten off.

Front
Work as for back until work measures 15 ins. to front opening.
Adjust length here.

Divide for front opening thus:

Left front
Work 31 (33–34) grps., 8 ch., turn.
Next row:
1 tr. into 4th ch. from hook, * 1 ch., leaving the last loop of each on hook, 1 tr. into same ch., miss 1 ch., 2 tr. into next ch., w.o.h. and draw through all loops on hook. Repeat from * once more, work in pattern to end, 3 ch., turn. (34 (36–37) grps.)
Work straight to hip (the same number of rows to correspond with back of dress to hip measurement).
Work darts as for back—side edge only—and insert pocket 3 ins. below waistline and 9 grps. from side edge.
Work to waist as for back. Mark with contrast wool. (29 (31–32) grps.)

Continue as for back to armhole shaping. (Left side.)

Armhole shaping
Sl. st. over 2 (2–3) grps. work in pattern to end, 3 ch., turn.
2nd row:
Pattern until 3 grps. remain, dec. 1 grp., 1 grp., 3 ch., turn.
3rd row:
Work in pattern, 3 ch., turn.

Repeat the last 2 rows 3 times more.

Continue straight until work measures 6 rows less than back to beginning of shoulder shaping ending at armhole edge.

Neck shaping
Work to within last 9 grps., dec. 1 grp., 1 grp., 3 ch., turn.
Work 1 row straight.
Next row:
Pattern to last 3 grps., dec. 1 grp., 1 grp., 3 ch., turn.
Next row:
1 grp., dec. 1 grp., pattern to end, 3 ch., turn.
Repeat the last 2 rows once more.

Shoulder shaping
Sl. st. over 4 (5–5) grps., omit starting ch., pattern to end. 3 ch., turn. Pattern over 6 (7–7) grps., turn, sl. st over 3 (3–3) grps., omit starting ch., pattern to end. Fasten off.
Mark left front for buttons evenly spaced leaving 6 ins. for rever.

Right front
Work as for left front reversing all shapings.

Buttonholes
Work buttonholes into the row corresponding with the markings for buttons on left front as follows: beginning at front edge of opening work 5 grps., 5 ch., turn, miss 3 grps., sl. st. into next grp., turn, 5 dc. over 5 ch. of buttonhole, sl. st. into top of grp., 1 ch., and continue in pattern to end, 3 ch., turn.

Next buttonhole row:
Pattern to buttonhole, 1 ch., leaving the last loop of each on

hook, 1 tr. into same grp., 2 tr. into first dc., w.o.h. and draw
through loops on hook, * 1 ch., 1 tr. into same grp., miss 1 dc.,
2 tr. into next dc., w.o.h. and draw through loops. Repeat from
* once more, 2 grps. to end, 3 ch., turn.

Sleeves
Make 74 (78–82) chain. (36 (38–40) grps.)
Work in pattern for 3 rows.
4th row:
Buttonhole row—work this as for 1st buttonhole row of front,
then continue in pattern to within last grp., 5 ch., turn, miss 3
grps., sl. st. into next grp., turn, 5 dc. over 5 ch., sl. st. into top
of grp., 1 ch., 1 grp., 3 ch., turn.
Next row:
1 tr. into first grp., * 1 ch., leaving last loop of each on hook,
1 tr. into same grp., 2 tr. into first dc., w.o.h. and draw through
all loops (miss 1 dc., 1 grp. into next dc.) twice * pattern to next
buttonhole 27 (29–31) grps.
Repeat from * to * pattern into next 2 grps. to end, 3 ch., turn.
Next row:
Work in pattern to end. Fasten off. (36 (38–40) grps.)
Next row:
Miss 18 (19–20) grps., join in wool into top of next grp., and
work 18 (19–20) grps. in pattern, continue on opposite side of cuff
to end, 3 ch., turn.
8th row:
2 grps., increase 1 grp. into ch. st. between grps., pattern to last
2 grps., increase between grps., 2 grps. to end, 3 ch., turn.
Work 7 rows straight.
16th row:
Increase 1 grp. at each end of row as before.
Repeat the last 8 rows twice more. (44 (46–48) grps.)
Work 5 rows straight or length desired to sleeve head.
Sleeve head
Sl. st. over 2 (2–3) grps., work to last 2 (2–3) grps, turn.
2nd row:
2 grps., dec. 1 grp., work to within last 3 grps., dec. 1 grp.,
pattern to end., 3 ch., turn.
Repeat this row 4 times more.
Decrease 1 grp. at the end of the following 10 rows.

Next row:
Dec. 1 grp. at each end of row.
Next row:
Sl. st. over 1 grp., pattern to last grp., turn.
Next row:
Sl. st. over 3 grps., pattern to last 3 grps. Fasten off.

Making up
Press each piece separately. Join shoulder seams thus—with right
sides facing, lay the two edges to be sewn side by side and
carefully draw the loops of each stitch together, turn to wrong side
and draw the remaining loops together. Press seams.
Join side seams in the same way matching rows. Sew back of
pockets to dress. Press side seams. Sew lower edges of front
opening neatly together on wrong side.

Collar
Join in wool at shoulder seam and work in pattern along back of
neck to opposite shoulder seam, sl. st. along 2 rows on neck, turn
and work in pattern to 2 rows past shoulder seam, sl. st. along
next 2 rows, turn. Continue in this way for 2 more rows until $1\frac{1}{2}$
ins are left for rever.
Work straight for $2\frac{1}{2}$ ins. Fasten off.

Sew in sleeves with a fine back stitch, 1 stitch in from edge.

Borders
Lower edge of dress: with right side facing, work 2 dc. into each
foundation ch., into which grp. has been worked, turn and work
1 sl. st. into each dc. taking care not to work sl. st. too tightly.
Fasten off.
Work the same border round sleeve ends and opening.

Front opening of dress: left side—with right side facing, join wool
at a point level with beginning of armhole shaping and work 2
dc. into each row end, turn and work 1 sl. st. into each dc.
Work the same border on right side of front opening beginning
at lower edge and ending at a point level with beginning of
armhole shaping.

Collar and revers: rejoin wool to left front edge with wrong side of work facing, and work border along edges of revers and collar.

Pocket tops: join in wool and work 4 rows of pattern along top of pocket. Turn over 2 rows of pattern to make pocket flap and work border of dc. and sl. st. along flap.

Darn in all loose ends neatly on wrong side.

Crochet buttons

Make 3 chain, join with sl. st. to form a ring.

1st round:

Work 6 dc. into ring, 2 ch.

2nd round:

12 tr. into centre of ring working over the dc. (or sufficient tr. until button front is well covered). Join with sl. st.

Next round:

1 dc. into each tr.

Next round:

1 dc. into each dc.

Insert button mould and draw up, leaving sufficient wool to sew button to dress.

Make link buttons for sleeve ends.

To strengthen collar

Thread a darning needle with wool double, fasten securely to shoulder at neck edge on wrong side of work and weave through the grps. to opposite shoulder, draw wool taut and fasten ends securely.

Chanel-type suit

MATERIALS

The original was made in Paton's Cameo Crepe Wool. If this is not available, a fine 4-ply crepe wool or synthetic yarn may be used. Approx. quantity—28 (30–32) ozs. or 16 (17–18) 50-gr. balls. Crochet hook size 3.00 (U.S. D).

Waist length 1-inch wide elastic. 1½ yards lining for skirt (optional).

Measurements

Skirt: To fit 36 (38–40) inch hip. Length 24 ins.

Coat: 34 (36–38) inch bust. Sleeve seam 14 ins. Length 22 ins.

Tension

3 grps. = 1 inch. 4 rows – 1½ ins.

METHOD
SKIRT

Back and front

Make 116 (122–128) chain.

1st row:

1 tr. into 4th ch. from hook, * 1 ch., leaving the last loop of each on hook, 1 tr. into same ch. as last tr., miss 1 ch., 2 tr. into next ch. (4 loops on hook), w.o.h. and draw through all loops on hook (1 grp. made). Repeat from * to end, 3 ch., turn. (57 (60–63) grps.)

2nd row:

(Right side) 1 tr. into top of first grp. (picking up 2 loops). * 1 ch., leaving the last loop of each on hook, 1 tr. into same grp., miss ch. st., 2 tr. into top of next grp. (picking up 2 loops) (4 loops on hook). W.o.h. and draw through all loops on hook.

Repeat from * to end working last 2 tr. into turning ch., 3 ch., turn.

Repeat 2nd row until 18 ins. have been worked or length desired to hip, 3 ch., turn.

Decrease for darts
Next row:
Work 9 grps. in pattern, * 1 ch., leaving the last loop of each on hook, 1 tr. into same grp., 1 tr. into next grp., 2 tr. into next grp. (5 loops on hook), w.o.h. and draw through all loops on hook. ** (1 grp. decreased) pattern to within last 11 grps.

Repeat from * to **, work in pattern to end, 3 ch., turn.
Work 1 row straight in pattern, 3 ch., turn.

Repeat last 2 rows 5 times more.

Work straight until work measures 24 ins. or length desired. Fasten off.

COAT
Back
Make 108 (114–120) chain.

Work in pattern on 53 (56–59) grps. until work measures 12 ins. or length desired to raglan shaping. 3 ch., turn.

Raglan shaping
1 tr. into first grp., * 1 ch., leaving the last loop of each on hook, 1 tr. into same grp., 1 tr. into next grp., 2 tr. into next grp. (5 loops on hook), w.o.h. and draw through all loops on hook, ** pattern to last 3 grps. Repeat from * to **, 1 grp., 3 ch., turn.
Next row:
Work straight in pattern, 3 ch., turn.

Repeat 1st and 2nd rows alternately 7 (6–7) times more and then decrease each end on every row 12 (14–14) times. 13 (14–15) grps. remain at back of neck. Fasten off. 28 (28–30) rows in raglan shaping.

Pockets (2)
Make 30 chain. (14 grps.)
Work in pattern for 10 rows. Fasten off.

Left front
Make 54 (58–62) chain. (26 (28–30) grps.)
Work in pattern as for back for 10 rows.

Pocket shaping
Front edge of coat. Pattern on 13 (14–15) grps., 3 ch., turn.
Next row:
1 tr. into first grp., 1 ch., leaving the last loop of each on hook, 1 tr. into same grp., 1 tr. into next grp., 2 tr. into next grp., w.o.h. and draw through all loops on hook, pattern to end, 3 ch., turn.
Next row:
Pattern to within last 3 grps., dec. 1 grp., pattern into last grp. Fasten off. Rejoin wool into ch. st. at the beginning of pocket shaping, 3 ch., and work in pattern to end, 3 ch., turn.
Next row:
Pattern to within last 3 grps., dec. 1 grp., pattern into last grp., 3 ch., turn.
Next row:
1 tr. into first grp., 1 ch., dec. 1 grp., pattern to end.

Insert pocket
Work in pattern for 6 (7–8) grps., then along the 14 grps. of pocket, miss 14 grps. on front and work remaining 6 (7–8) grps. on front, 3 ch., turn.

Work straight in pattern until front has the same number of rows as back to raglan shaping.

Raglan shaping
Front edge of coat: Pattern to last 3 grps., dec. 1 grp., pattern into last grp., 3 ch., turn.
Next row:
Work straight in pattern, 3 ch., turn.
Repeat these two rows 7 (5–5) times more and then decrease on every row at raglan end 7 (11–13) times, 3 ch., turn.

Neck shaping
Raglan edge: dec. 1 grp. for raglan, work to within last 3 grps., 3 ch., turn.
Next row:
Dec. 1 grp., pattern to last 3 grps., dec. 1 grp., 1 grp., 3 ch., turn.
Repeat this row twice more. (1 grp. remains.)

Right front
Work as for left front reversing all shapings.

Sleeves
Sleeve ends: Make 28 (30–32) chain. (13 (14–15) grps.)
1st row:
Work in pattern to end, 3 ch., turn.
2nd row:
Pattern to last 2 grps., increase 1 grp. into ch. st. between grps., pattern into 2 grps., 3 ch., turn.
3rd row:
Work straight in pattern, 3 ch., turn.
4th row:
As 2nd row. Fasten off.
Work another piece in this way, reversing shapings, 3 ch., turn.
Next row:
Work in pattern to end of row and then along second piece, thus joining the 2 halves of sleeve ends together. (30 (32–34) grps.)

Next row:
Work straight in pattern, 3 ch., turn.
Next row:
Pattern into 2 grps., increase 1 grp., pattern to last 2 grps.,
increase 1 grp., 2 grps., 3 ch., turn.
Work 4 rows straight in pattern.
Repeat the last 5 rows 4 times more, then work straight until work
measures 14 ins. or length desired to raglan shaping.

Raglan shaping
Work the first 2 rows of raglan shaping for back. Repeat these 2
rows 9 (9–10) times more and then decrease each end on every
row 8 (8–8) times, 4 (6–8) grps. remain at top of sleeve. Fasten off.
28 (28–30) rows in raglan shaping.

Making up
Press each piece separately on the wrong side.

Skirt
There are two ways of joining crochet seams:
A. The double crochet method.
B. A 'flat' seam.
Personally, I think it depends on the crochet stitch one is using
and for this stitch, I would suggest the 'flat' seam as follows:
With right sides facing, lay the two edges to be sewn side by side
and carefully draw the loops of each stitch together. Press seams
lightly.

Border
Lower edge of skirt.
With right side facing, work 2 dc. into each foundation ch. into
which grp. has been worked, turn, and work 1 sl. st. into each dc.
taking care not to work sl. st. too tightly.

Waistline
Join elastic to fit waist measurement, pin to skirt, distributing
fullness evenly. Sew with wool, using a herringbone stitch, catching
elastic above and below as you work to prevent elastic rolling.

Coat

Join raglan seams matching rows. Press seams lightly. Join side seams and sew back of pockets to fronts of coat. Press side seams.

Border

For front of pocket.

With right side facing, rejoin wool and work 1 row dc. along pocket, turn, and 1 sl. st. into each dc. Fasten off.

Braid trimming

For border round edges of coat.

Beginning at side seam of left front and with wrong side of garment facing, rejoin wool and work 3 ch., * 1 grp. into foundation ch. into which grp. has been worked. Repeat from * to corner of right front, 1 ch., 1 tr. into same foundation ch., continuing up right front, 1 tr. into first row end, 2 tr. into 2nd row end (5 loops on hook) w.o.h. and draw through all loops on hook (dec. made). 1 grp. into each row end to neck shaping, dec. 1 grp. at corner, 1 grp. into each grp. round neck shaping, dec. 1 grp. at corner, work down left front to correspond with right front, dec. 1 grp. at corner, and work along lower edge to correspond, join with sl. st. Fasten off. Turn border up on to right side of coat and with right side facing rejoin wool on the outside edge of border between grps. and work * 3 ch., 1 dc. into 3rd ch. from hook, sl. st. into space between next 2 grps. Repeat from * all round. Fasten off.

Work a further row of picots round the inner edge of border. Join with sl. st. Fasten off.

Using 1 strand of wool, blind stitch braid to coat.
Work braid trimming round sleeve ends.
Darn all loose ends in neatly on wrong side.

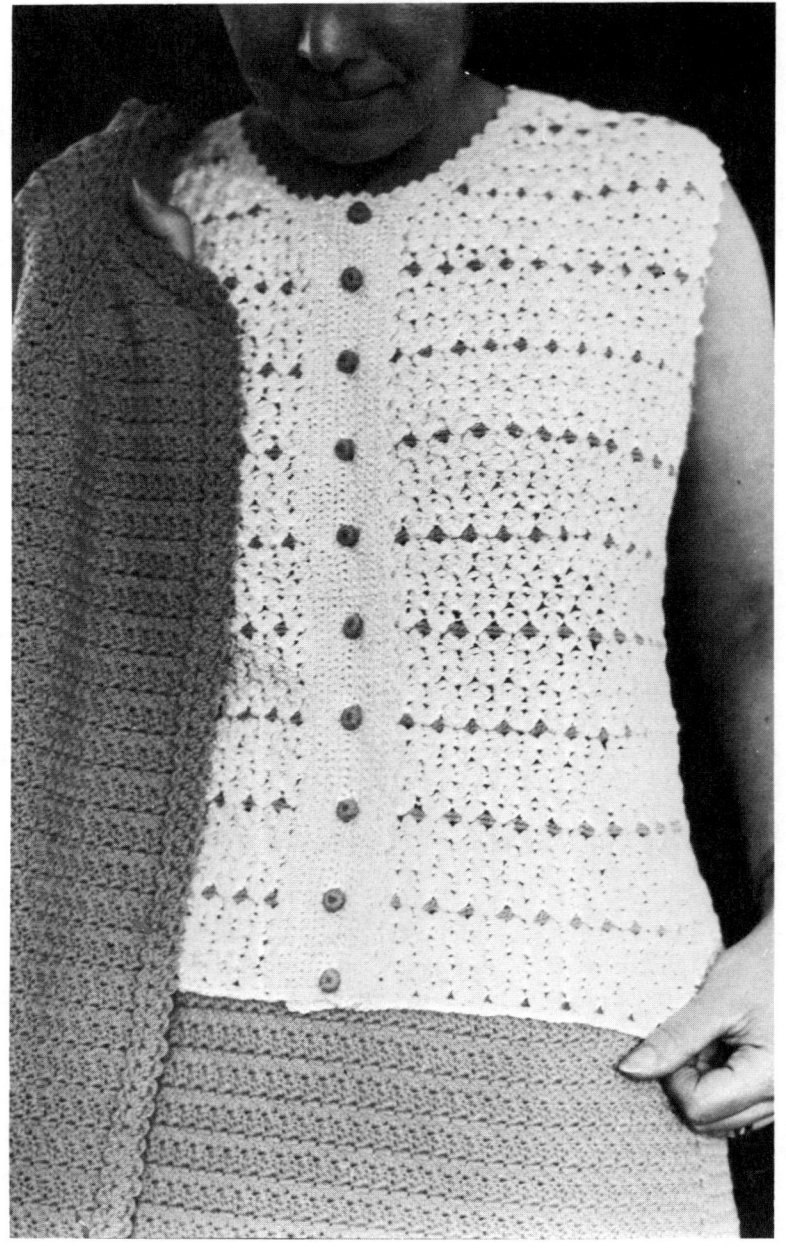

Sleeveless blouse for Chanel-type suit

MATERIALS

9 (10–10) ozs. or 5 50-gr. balls Lister's Star Spun in White.
Approx. $\frac{3}{4}$ oz. contrast wool as used for suit. Crochet hook size
2.50 (U.S. C). Pure crepe wool (4-ply) in white with silver thread
incorporated would be a good substitute.

Measurements

To fit 34 (36–38) ins. bust size. Length from shoulder 20 ins.

Tension

5 groups = 3 ins. 5 rows = 1½ ins.

METHOD

Back

Make 112 (120–128) chain.

1st row:

Leaving the last loop of each tr., on hook, 2 tr. into 4th ch. from hook (3 loops on hook), w.o.h. and draw through all loops on hook (½ grp. made). 3 ch., leaving the last loop of each tr. on hook, 3 tr. into same ch. as last grp. (4 loops on hook), w.o.h. and draw through all loops on hook. (These 3 tr., 3 ch., and 3 tr form 1 grp.) * miss 3 ch., 1 grp. into next ch. Repeat from * to end. (28 (30–32) grps.)

2nd row:

3 ch. (this forms first tr. of ½ grp.), 2 tr. into top of first ½ grp., * miss 3 ch., (½ grp., 3 ch. and ½ grp.) into top of next ½ grp. (this gives a complete grp. between the grps. on previous row. Repeat from * ending with miss 3 ch., ½ grp. into top of last ½ grp., turn. 27 (29–31) grps. and ½ grp. at each end of row.)

3rd row:

3 ch., 1 grp. into top of first ½ grp., * miss 3 ch., 1 grp. into top of next ½ grp. Repeat from * ending with miss 3 ch., 1 grp. into top of last ½ grp. (28 (30–32) grps.)

Repeat 2nd and 3rd rows once more. Do not turn at end of 5th row.

6th row:

Drop loop from hook. Join contrast wool into top of first ½ grp. at beginning of previous row (right side of work facing) and work 2 ch., 3 dc. over 3 ch. space, * 2 dc. into top of ½ grp., 3 dc. over 3 ch. space. Repeat from * to end and draw dropped loop of main wool through hook, turn. Break off contrast wool.

7th row:

3 ch., ½ grp. into top of first ½ grp. * miss 3 dc., 1 grp. over 2 dc. into top of ½ grp. of previous row (this forms a spot). Repeat from * ending with ½ grp. over 2 dc. into top of last ½ grp. of previous row. Turn.

Work a further 4 rows in pattern ending last row with miss 3 ch., ½ grp. into last ½ grp. (4 loops on hook), drop main wool and draw contrast wool through 4 loops on hook. *Do not break off main wool.*

12th row:

Contrast wool—right side facing—2 ch., 2 dc. into top of first ½ grp. * 3 dc. over 3 ch. space, 2 dc. into top of next ½ grp. Repeat from * to end. Break off contrast wool. *Do not turn.*

13th row:

Pick up main colour at beginning of previous row and draw through top of first ½ grp., 3 ch., 1 grp. over 2 dc. into top of ½ grp. of previous row. * miss 3 dc., 1 grp. over 2 dc. into top of next ½ grp. of previous row. Repeat from * to end.

Work 2 rows straight in pattern.

Begin shaping darts

16th row:

3 ch., ½ grp. into top of first ½ grp., 6 (7–8) grps., miss 3 ch., ½ grp. into top of next ½ grp. (½ grp. decreased), 13 grps., miss 3 ch., ½ grp. into top of next ½ grp. (another ½ grp., dec.) 6 (7–8) grps., miss 3 ch., ½ grp. into top of last ½ grp.

17th row:

2nd dec. row: 6 (7–8) grps., 1 grp. into top of next ½ grp., 12 grps., 1 grp. into top of next ½ grp., 6 (7–8) grps., to end. *Do not turn.*

18th row:

With contrast wool, repeat 6th row.

19th row:

Repeat 7th row.

Work 2 rows straight in pattern.

22nd row:

3rd dec. row. 3 ch., 6 (7–8) grps., miss 3 ch., ½ grp., into top of next ½ grp., 12 grps., miss 3 ch., ½ grp. into top of next ½ grp., 6 (7–8) grps. to end.

23rd row:

4th dec. row. 3 ch., ½ grp. into top of first ½ grp., 5 (6–7) grps., 1 grp. into top of ½ grp., 11 grps., 1 grp. into top of ½ grp., 5 (6–7) grps., miss 3 ch., ½ grp. into top of last ½ grp. 24 (26–28) grps.

24th row:

With contrast wool repeat 12th row.

25th row.

Repeat 13th row.

Work 2 rows straight in pattern.

28th row:

Increase row. 3 ch., $\frac{1}{2}$ grp. into top of first $\frac{1}{2}$ grp., 5 (6–7) grps., miss 3 ch., ($\frac{1}{2}$ grp., 2 ch., $\frac{1}{2}$ grp., 2 ch. and $\frac{1}{2}$ grp.) into top of next $\frac{1}{2}$ grp. (increase made), 11 grps. miss 3 ch., ($\frac{1}{2}$ grp., 2 ch., $\frac{1}{2}$ grp., 2 ch. and $\frac{1}{2}$ grp.) into top of next $\frac{1}{2}$ grp., 5 (6–7) grps., miss 3 ch., $\frac{1}{2}$ grp. into top of last $\frac{1}{2}$ grp.

29th row:

2nd inc. row. 3 ch., 6 (7–8) grps., 1 grp. into top of centre $\frac{1}{2}$ grp. of inc., 12 grps., 1 grp. into top of centre $\frac{1}{2}$ grp. of inc., 6 (7–8) grps. 26 (28–30) grps.

30th row:

With contrast wool repeat 6th row.

31st row:

Repeat 7th row.

Work 2 rows straight in pattern.

34th row:

3rd inc. row. 3 ch., 6 (7–8) grps., miss 3 ch., ($\frac{1}{2}$ grp., 2 ch., $\frac{1}{2}$ grp., 2 ch. and $\frac{1}{2}$ grp.) into top of next $\frac{1}{2}$ grp., 12 grps., miss 3 ch., increase into top of next $\frac{1}{2}$ grp., 6 (7–8) grps. to end.

35th row:

4th inc. row: 3 ch., $\frac{1}{2}$ grp. into top of first $\frac{1}{2}$ grp., 6 (7–8) grps., 1 grp. into top of centre $\frac{1}{2}$ grp. of inc., 13 grps., 1 grp., into top of centre $\frac{1}{2}$ grp. of inc., 6 (7–8) grps., miss 3 ch., $\frac{1}{2}$ grp. into top of last $\frac{1}{2}$ grp. (28 (30–32) grps.)

36th row:

With contrast wool repeat 12th row.

37th row:

Repeat 13th row.

Work 2 rows straight in pattern.

Shaping armholes

Sl. st. over 2 grps., $\frac{1}{2}$ grp. into next grp., 23 (25–27) grps., miss 3 ch., $\frac{1}{2}$ grp. into top of next grp., turn.

41st row:
3 ch., work in pattern, decreasing $\frac{1}{2}$ grp. at beginning and end of row.
42nd row:
With contrast wool, repeat 6th row.
43rd row:
Repeat 7th row, dec. $\frac{1}{2}$ grp. at each end of row.
44th row:
Work in pattern, dec. $\frac{1}{2}$ grp. at each end of row.
Work 3 rows straight in pattern.
48th row:
With contrast wool, repeat 12th row.
49th row:
Repeat 13th row.
Work 4 rows straight in pattern.
54th row:
With contrast wool, repeat 6th row.
55th row:
Repeat 7th row. 21 (23–25) grps.
Work 4 rows straight in pattern.
60th row:
With contrast wool, repeat 12th row.
61st row:
Repeat 13th row.
Work 1 row straight in pattern.
Next row:
3 ch., 1 grp. into top of first $\frac{1}{2}$ grp., * miss 3 ch., 1 grp. into top of next $\frac{1}{2}$ grp. Repeat from * ending with miss 3 ch., 1 grp. into top of last $\frac{1}{2}$ grp.

Shoulder shaping
Sl. st. over 3 grps., work to within last 3 grps., sl. st. into next st., turn.
Next row:
Sl. st. over 3 grps., work to within last 3 grps., sl. st. into next st. Fasten off.

Left front
Make 56 (60–64) chain. (14 (15–16) grps.)
Work as given for back until 15 rows have been completed.

Begin shaping darts
16th row:
3 ch., ½ grp. into top of first ½ grp. 5 (6–7) grps., miss 3 ch., ½
grp. into top of next ½ grp. (½ grp. dec.) 7 (7–7) grps., miss 3 ch.,
½ grp. into top of last ½ grp.
17th row:
3 ch., 7 (7–7) grps., 1 grp. into top of next ½ grp., 5 (6–7) grps.
to end.
18th row:
Repeat 6th row of back.
19th row:
Repeat 7th row of back.
Work 2 rows straight in pattern.
22nd row:
3rd dec. row: 3 ch., 7 (7–7) grps., miss 3 ch., ½ grp. into top of
next ½ grp., 5 (6–7) grps. to end.
23rd row:
4th dec. row: 3 ch., ½ grp. into top of first ½ grp., 4 (5–6) grps.,
1 grp. into top of next ½ grp., 6 (6–6) grps., miss 3 ch., ½ grp.
into top of last ½ grp. 12 (13–14) grps.
24th row:
With contrast wool, repeat 12th row of back.
25th row:
Repeat 13th row of back.
Work 2 rows straight in pattern.
28th row:
Increase row: 3 ch., ½ grp. into top of first ½ grp., 4 (5–6) grps.,
miss 3 ch., (½ grp., 2 ch., ½ grp., 2 ch. and ½ grp.) into next ½ grp.
(increase made), 6 (6–6) grps., miss 3 ch., ½ grp. into top of last
½ grp.
29th row:
2nd inc. row: 3 ch., 7 (7–7) grps., 1 grp. into top of centre ½ grp.
of inc. 5 (6–7) grps. to end. 13 (14–15) grps.
30th row:
With contrast wool, repeat 6th row of back.
31st row:
Repeat 7th row of back.
Work 2 rows straight in pattern.

34th row:
3rd inc. row: 3 ch., 7 (7–7) grps., miss 3 ch., increase into next
$\frac{1}{2}$ grp., 5 (6–7) grps. to end.
35th row:
4th inc. row: 3 ch., $\frac{1}{2}$ grp. into top of first $\frac{1}{2}$ grp., 5 (6–7) grps.,
1 grp. into top of centre $\frac{1}{2}$ grp. of inc., 7 (7–7) grps., miss 3 ch.,
$\frac{1}{2}$ grp. into top of last $\frac{1}{2}$ grp. 14 (15–16) grps.
36th row:
With contrast wool, repeat 12th row of back.
37th row:
Repeat 13th row of back.
Work 2 rows straight in pattern.

Armhole shaping
Sl. st. over 2 grps., 3 ch., $\frac{1}{2}$ grp. into top of next $\frac{1}{2}$ grp., * miss
3 ch., 1 grp. into top of next $\frac{1}{2}$ grp. Repeat from * ending with
miss 3 ch., $\frac{1}{2}$ grp. into top of last $\frac{1}{2}$ grp.
41st row:
3 ch., 11 (12–13) grps., miss 3 ch., $\frac{1}{2}$ grp. into top of last $\frac{1}{2}$ grp.
42nd row:
With contrast wool, repeat 6th row of back.
43rd row:
Repeat 7th row of back, decreasing $\frac{1}{2}$ grp. at armhole edge.
44th row:
Work in pattern, dec. $\frac{1}{2}$ grp. at armhole edge. (10 (11–12) grps.)
Work 3 rows straight in pattern.
48th row:
With contrast wool, repeat 12th row of back.
49th row:
Repeat 13th row of back.
Work 3 rows straight in pattern.

Neck shaping
Armhole edge. Work to within last grp., turn.
54th row:
With contrast wool, repeat 6th row of back.
55th row:
Repeat 7th row of back, decreasing $\frac{1}{2}$ grp. at neck edge.
Work 4 more rows, dec. $\frac{1}{2}$ grp. at neck edge on every row, keeping
armhole edge straight.

60th row:
With contrast wool, repeat 12th row of back.
61st row:
Repeat 13th row of back dec. $\frac{1}{2}$ grp. at neck edge.
62nd row:
Dec. $\frac{1}{2}$ grp. at neck edge, work in pattern to end.
63rd row:
Increase $\frac{1}{2}$ grp. at armhole edge, work in pattern to end.

Shoulder shaping
Work in pattern to last 3 grps., sl. st. into next st., turn.
Next row:
Sl. st. over 2 grps., work to end. Fasten off.

Right front
Work as for left front reversing dart, armhole, neck and shoulder shapings.
Darn loose ends in carefully on wrong side.
Press each piece separately under a dry cloth.

Front borders
Left front:
With white and right side facing, rejoin wool to neck edge and work, 2 dc. into each tr. row end, 1 dc. into each contrast wool end to lower edge of front, 2 ch., turn.
Next row:
1 dc. into each dc., 2 ch., turn. Work a further 11 rows in dc. Fasten off.
Right front:
With right side facing, rejoin wool to lower edge and work 6 rows dc. as for left front.
Next row:
Buttonhole row: 1 dc., 3 ch., miss 3 dc., 1 dc. into next 6 dc., * 4 ch., miss 4 dc., 1 dc. into next 7 dc. Repeat from * 6 times more, 4 ch., miss 4 dc., dc. into each st. to end., 2 ch., turn.
Next row:
In dc., working 4 dc. over each 4 ch. space, 2 ch., turn.
Work a further 5 rows dc. Fasten off.
With right side of work facing, work a row of picots along right front edge thus:

Rejoin wool, * 3 ch., 1 dc. into 3rd ch. from hook, miss 2 dc., sl. st. into next dc., repeat from * to end. Fasten off.

Join shoulder and side seams
Join together using the dc. method.

Border for lower edge of blouse
Rejoin wool to lower edge of left front, right side facing, and work 1 dc. into each row end of border, 1 dc. into base of first grp., * 3 dc. into next 3 ch. loop., 1 dc. into base of next grp. Repeat from * to last grp. 1 dc. into each row end of border, turn.
Next row:
1 sl. st. into each dc. taking care not to work too tightly. Fasten off.

Armhole border
With right side facing, work a row dc. evenly, having one less dc. at each side of shoulder seam, join with sl. st. and without turning, work a row of picots into dc. Fasten off.

Neck edge
With right side facing, rejoin wool at neck edge of right front and work, 1 dc. into each of 5 row ends of border, 4 ch., miss 4 row ends of dc. 1 dc. into 4 remaining row ends of border, dc. evenly all round neck, 13 dc. into border on left front, 2 ch., turn.
Next row:
1 dc. into each dc., working 4 dc. over 4 ch. space of buttonhole, 3 ch., turn.
Next row:
Work a row of picots up to beginning of left front border. Fasten off.

Crochet buttons
Using a fine crochet hook size 2.00 (U.S. B) make 3 chain and join with sl. st. to form a ring. Work 6 dc. into ring, join with sl. st.
Next round:
12 dc. into centre of ring (over the dc. of previous round). Break off wool leaving sufficient to sew button to garment. Thread wool into tapestry needle and draw up button, stuffing button firmly with scraps of wool.

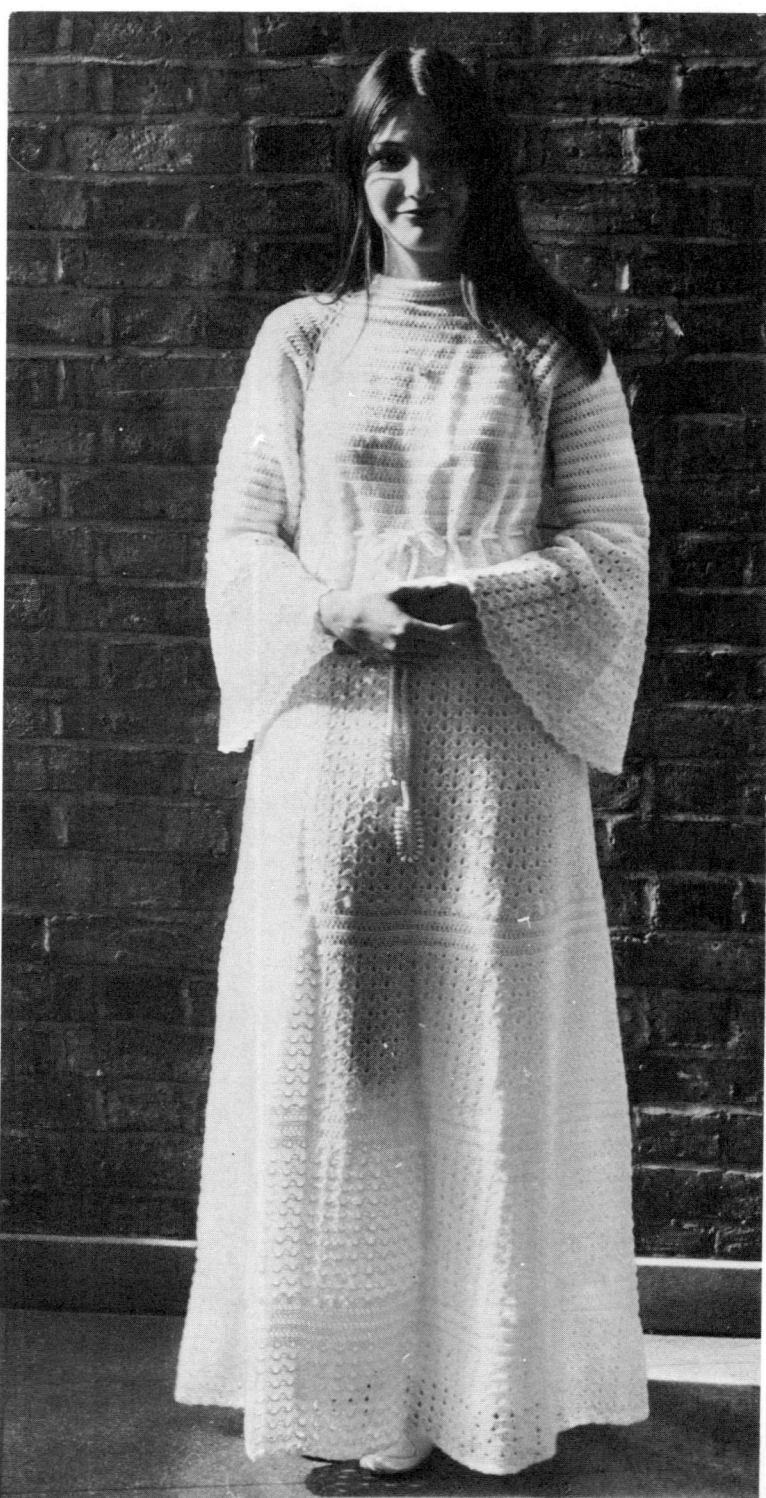

Wedding dress

This simple style wedding dress is easy to make—there are no seams to join. It is adaptable for any length as I begin this dress at the neck and work down to the hemline.

It is also adaptable for different types of yarn. In addition to the wool used in this dress, it can also be made with Jaeger's 'Dappel Crepe Courtelle' using a size 2.50 crochet hook (U.S. C). This pattern also makes an elegant dinner gown in either Lister's 'Star Spun' or Sirdar 'After Six' using crochet hook size 2.50. The dress has also been made up successfully as a dinner gown in a fine 4-ply synthetic yarn, using about 27 ozs. or 17 40-gr. balls of synthetic yarn.

MATERIALS
3C ozs. Sirdar Wool 3-ply. Crochet hook size 3.00 (U.S. D). 19 pearl buttons for back of dress. Pearls to trim braid for girdle.

Measurements
To fit 34–36 inch bust size. To make a smaller size use crochet hook size 2.50 (U.S. C).

Tension
Yoke: 5 trs. = 1 inch. 3 rows = 1 inch. Skirt: 4 grps. = 3 ins. 5 grp. rows = 3 ins.

METHOD
Beginning at yoke make 86 chain.

1st row:

1 tr. into 4th ch. from hook, 1 tr. into next 11 ch., ** 2 ch., 1 dc. into next ch. and pull up loop on hook to ½ inch; * insert hook into same ch. pull loop through, w.o.h. and draw through 1 loop on hook, pull loop up to ½ inch (chain st. made). Repeat from * 4 times more (6 loops on hook), insert hook once more into same ch. pull loop through, w.o.h. and draw through 1 loop but do not pull this st. up. Slip the 6 loops off back end of hook leaving the last ch. st. on hook ** (These 6 loops will be picked up in the following row.) 1 group made. 2 ch., 1 tr. into each of next 14 ch. Repeat from ** to **, 2 ch., 1 tr. into each of next 26 ch. Repeat from ** to **, 2 ch., 1 tr. into each of next 14 ch. Repeat from ** to **, 2 ch., 1 tr. into each of next 12 ch., 3 ch., turn.

2nd row:

(Twin Tr.) Miss first tr., 1 tr. into next tr. * leaving the last loop of each tr. on hook, 1 tr. into same tr. as last tr., 1 tr. into next tr. (3 loops on hook), w.o.h. and draw through all loops on hook (twin tr.). Repeat from * to first grp., 1 tr. into 2 ch. space, 2 ch., sl. st. into each of first 3 loops of grp., 3 ch., sl. st. into each of next 3 loops, 2 ch., 1 tr. into 2 ch. space, tw. tr. into next 14 trs., 1 tr. into 2 ch. space, 2 ch., sl. st. into each of 3 loops of grp., 3 ch., sl. st. into each of next 3 loops, 2 ch., 1 tr. into 2 ch. space, tw. tr. into each of next 26 tr., 1 tr. into 2 ch. space, 2 ch., sl.

st. into 3 loops, 3 ch., sl. st. into next 3 loops, 2 ch., 1 tr. into
2 ch. space, tw. tr. into next 14 tr., 1 tr. into 2 ch. space, 2 ch.,
sl. st. into each of 3 loops, 3 ch., sl. st. into next 3 loops, 2 ch.,
1 tr. into 2 ch. space, tw. tr. into each tr. to end, 1 tr. into turning
ch., 3 ch., turn.

3rd row:

Miss the first tw. tr., 1 tr. into each tw. tr. to grp., 1 tr. into 2
ch. space, 2 ch., grp. into 3 ch. space of grp. on previous row,
2 ch., 1 tr. into 2 ch. space, 1 tr. into each tw. tr. to next grp.
1 tr. into 2 ch. space, 2 ch., grp. into 3 ch. space of grp., 2 ch.,
1 tr. into 2 ch. space, 1 tr. into each of next 28 tw. tr., 1 tr. into
2 ch. space, 2 ch., grp. into 3 ch. space of grp., 2 ch., 1 tr. into
2 ch. space, 1 tr. into each tw. tr. to next grp., 1 tr. into 2 ch.
space, 2 ch., grp. into grp., 2 ch., 1 tr. into 2 ch. space., 1 tr.
into each tw. tr. to end, 1 tr. into turning ch., 3 ch., turn.

4th row:

Miss first tr., tw. tr. into each tr. to grp. * 1 tr. into space, 2 ch.,
sl. st. into each of 3 loops of grp., 3 ch., sl. st. into each of next
3 loops, 2 ch., 1 tr. into space, tw. tr. into each tr. to grp. Repeat
from * twice ending with 1 tr. into space, 2 ch., sl. st. into each
of 3 loops, 3 ch., sl. st. into each of next 3 loops, 2 ch., 1 tr.
into space, tw. tr. to end, 1 tr. into turning ch., 3 ch., turn.

Repeat the last 2 rows, increasing 1 tr. into 2 ch. space each side
of grps. as before on every row for 22 more rows ending with tw.
tr. row. (76 tw. tr. on front—37 tw. tr. on each side of back—64
tr. on each shoulder.)

27th row:

Miss first tr., 17 tr., 2 tr. into next tr., 18 tr., 1 tr. into 2 ch. space,
2 ch., grp. into 3 ch. space of grp., 2 ch., miss 64 tw. tr. on
shoulder, grp. into 3 ch. space of grp., 2 ch., 1 tr. into 2 ch.
space, 19 tr., 2 tr. into next tr., 36 tr., 2 tr. into next tr., 19 tr.,
1 tr. into space, 2 ch., grp. into 3 ch. space of grp., 2 ch., miss
64 tw. tr., grp. into 3 ch. space of grp., 1 tr. into space, 18 tr., 2
tr. into next tr., 18 tr., 3 ch., turn.

28th row:

Tw. tr. along back (1 sl. st. into each of next 6 loops), twice, tw.
tr. along front (sl. st. into each of next 6 loops), twice, tw. tr.
along back, 3 ch., turn.

29th row:
1 tr. into each tw. tr. along back (miss 1 loop, 1 tr. into next
loop), 6 times, 1 tr. into each tw. tr. along front (miss 1 loop, 1
tr. into next loop), 6 times, 1 tr. into each tw. tr. along back, 3
ch., turn.

Work straight in tw. tr. and tr. rows for a further 3 rows or length
desired ending with tw. tr. row. Join backs together with sl. st.
Turn, omitting turning chain.

Skirt
1st row:
2 ch., 1 grp. into first tw. tr., 2 ch., * miss 2 tw. tr., grp. into
next tw. tr., 2 ch. Repeat from * ending with 1 grp. into last tw.
tr., 3 ch., turn. (58 grps.)
2nd row:
Sl. st. into each of first 3 loops, 3 ch., * sl. st. into each of next
2 loops, insert hook into last loop of grp. and into the first loop
of next grp., w.o.h. and draw through all loops on hook (2 loops
sl. st'd together), sl. st. into each of next 2 loops, 3 ch. Repeat
from * ending with sl. st. into each of last 3 loops, sl. st. into top
of first grp., 3 ch., turn.
3rd row:
1 grp. into 3 ch. space of first grp., 2 ch., * 1 grp. into 3 ch. space
of next grp., 2 ch. Repeat from * to end, turn.
4th row:
Repeat 2nd row.
Repeat the last 2 rows 9 times more, joining rows together on
each 2nd round.
23rd row:
(Increase row) Work 7 grps., increase 1 grp. between grps., 15
grps., inc. 1 grp. between grps., 14 grps., inc. 1 grp., 15 grps.,
inc. 1 grp., 7 grps., turn. (62 grps.)
Next row and each alternate row: Repeat 2nd row.
Now work 4 rows grps. straight. (8 rows in all including sl. st.
rows.)
Next row:
(2nd inc. row.) Work 8 grps., inc. 1 grp., 15 grps., inc. 1 grp., 16
grps., inc. 1 grp., 15 grps., inc. 1 grp., 8 grps., turn. (66 grps.)
Work 4 rows grps. straight.

3rd inc. row:

9 grps., inc. 1 grp., 15 grps., inc. 1 grp., 18 grps., inc. 1 grp.,
15 grps., inc. 1 grp., 9 grps. turn. (70 grps.)
Work 3 rows grps. straight. (25 rows grps. from beginning of
skirt.) Do not turn.

Twin tr. and tr. band
1st row:

With wrong side of work facing, work in tw. tr. thus:
Sl. st. back in between grps., 3 ch., leaving the last loop of each
on hook, 1 tr. between grps., 1 tr. into next 3 ch. space, w.o.h.
and draw through 3 loops on hook; * tw. tr. into same 3 ch.
space, 1 tr. into same space again and 1 tr. between next 2 grps.,
w.o.h. and draw through 3 loops on hook, 1 tr. into same place
between grps., and 1 tr. into next 3 ch. space. w.o.h. and draw
through 3 loops on hook. Repeat from * to end, join with sl. st.,
3 ch., turn.

2nd row of band:

1 tr. into each tw. tr. increasing 12 tr. evenly along the row, join
with sl. st., 3 ch., turn.

3rd row:

Tw. tr. into each tr. Join with sl. st., 3 ch., turn.

4th row:

1 tr. into each tw. tr. to end, join with sl. st., 3 ch., turn.

5th and 7th rows:

Repeat the 3rd row.

6th row:

Repeat the 4th row.

Next row:

1 grp. into first tw. tr. * miss 2 tw. tr. 1 grp. into next tw. tr.
Repeat from * ending with 1 grp. into last tw. tr., turn. (74 grps.)

Next row:

Sl. st. row, join, 3 ch., turn.

5th increase row:

11 grps., inc. 1 grp., 15 grps., inc. 1 grp., 22 grps., inc. 1 grp.,
15 grps., inc. 1 grp., 11 grps., turn. (78 grps.)
Work 4 rows grps. straight.

6th inc. row:

12 grps., inc. 1 grp., 15 grps., inc. 1 grp., 24 grps., inc. 1 grp.,
15 grps., inc. 1 grp., 12 grps. turn. (82 grps.)

Work 4 rows grps. straight.

Repeat the first 5 rows of twin tr. and tr. band.

Next row:

1 grp. into first tw. tr. * miss 2 tw. tr. 1 grp. into next tw. tr.
Repeat from * ending with 1 grp. into last tw. tr., turn. (86 grps.)

8th inc. row:

14 grps., inc. 1 grp., 15 grps. inc. 1 grp., 28 grps. inc. 1 grp.,
15 grps. inc. 1 grp., 14 grps. turn. (90 grps.)

Work 4 grp. rows straight.

9th inc. row:

15 grps. inc. 1 grp., 15 grps. inc. 1 grp., 30 grps. inc. 1 grp., 15
grps. inc. 1 grp., 15 grps. turn. (94 grps.)

Work 4 grp. rows straight.

3rd twin tr. and tr. band:

Work as for first band.

Next row:

1 grp. into first tw. tr., * miss 2 tw. tr., 1 grp. into next tw. tr.
Repeat from * ending with 1 grp. into last tw. tr., turn. (98 grps.)

10th inc. row:

17 grps. inc. 1 grp., 15 grps. inc. 1 grp., 34 grps. inc. 1 grp., 15
grps. inc. 1 grp., 17 grps., turn. (102 grps.)

Work 3 grp. rows straight.

11th inc. row:

18 grps. inc. 1 grp., 15 grps. inc. 1 grp., 36 grps. inc. 1 grp., 15
grps. inc. 1 grp., 18 grps., turn. (106 grps.)

Work 2 grp. rows straight.

Next row:

Work the first row of twin tr. and tr. band. Fasten off.

Sleeves

With right side facing.

Left

Rejoin wool at armhole and work 65 tr., join with sl. st., 3 ch.,
turn.

2nd row:

Tw. tr. into each tr., join with sl. st., 3 ch., turn.

3rd row:

1 tr. into each tw. tr. decreasing 1 tr. at each end of row, join,
3 ch., turn.

Work 3 rows straight.

Repeat the last 4 rows 3 times more. (57 tw. tr.)

1st row grps.:

1 grp. into first tw. tr. * miss 2 tw. tr. 1 grp. into next tw. tr.
Repeat from * 8 times miss 1 tw. tr. 1 grp. into next tw. tr.,
(miss 2 tw. tr. 1 grp. into next tw. tr.), 9 times. (20 grps.)

2nd grp. row:

(5 grps., inc. between grps.) 3 times, 5 grps. (23 grps.)

Work 2 grp. rows straight.

5th grp. row:

(6 grps. inc. 1 grp.) twice, 5 grps. inc. 1 grp. 6 grps. (26 grps.)

Work 2 rows straight.

8th grp. row:

7 grps. inc. 1 grp. (6 grps. inc. 1 grp.), twice, 7 grps., turn. Work
2 rows straight.

11th grp. row:

8 grps. inc. 1 grp., 7 grps. inc. 1 grp., 6 grps. inc. 1 grp., 8 grps.,
turn. Work 2 rows straight.

14th grp. row:

9 grps. inc. 1 grp., 7 grps. inc. 1 grp., 7 grps. inc. 1 grp., 9 grps.
35 grps.

Work 2 rows straight.

Next row:

Sl. st. row. Fasten off.

Right

Work as for left reversing increase shapings.

Collar

Rejoin wool at back and work 74 tw. tr. all round neck, 3 ch., turn.

2nd row:

1 tr. into each tw. tr. 3 ch., turn.

Work a further 4 rows ending with tr. row. Omit turning chain
and do not turn.

Next row:

Working from left to right, 1 dc. into each tr. Fasten off.

Press dress *very lightly.*

With right side facing, work 2 dc. into each tr. row and around
back opening, turn and work 1 sl. st. into each dc. Fasten off.
Using the treble row ends for buttonholes—with one strand of
wool, buttonhole round these to strengthen. Sew buttons on
opposite side of back.

Girdle cord

Using double wool throughout, make 2 chain and work 1 dc. into 2nd ch. from hook, turn. Insert hook into the 2 loops at side, w.o.h. and draw through 2 loops; w.o.h. and draw through remaining 2 loops. * Turn. There are now 4 loops at side—insert hook into these 4 loops, w.o.h. and draw through 4 loops, w.o.h. and draw through remaining 4 loops. Repeat from * until cord measures approx. 60 ins. or length desired. Press lightly and thread cord through the first row of skirt beginning at front of dress. Trim ends with pearls and fasten into a bow.

Christening robe and coat

MATERIALS

7 ozs. Sirdar Majestic Wool 2-ply. This was used for the original
but any 2-ply pure wool may be used. 8 25-gr. balls will equal

about 7 ozs. Crochet hook size 2.50 (U.S. C). 7 Vogue baby
buttons for robe. 2 yards ½-inch wide ribbon for coat (optional).

Measurements
To fit 18-inch chest. Robe: length 25 ins. Sleeve seam 2 ins. Coat:
length 10 ins. Sleeve seam 4 ins.

METHOD

ROBE
Beginning at neck. The yoke is worked in 1 row treble and 1 row
twin treble.
Make 68 chain.
1st row:
1 tr. into 4th ch. from hook, 1 tr. into each of next 8 ch., 3 tr.
into next ch.; 1 tr. into each of next 11 ch., 3 tr. into next ch.;
1 tr. into each of next 20 ch., 3 tr. into next ch.; 1 tr. into each
of next 11 ch., 3 tr. into next ch.; 1 tr. into each of last 10 ch.,
3 ch., turn.
2nd row:
Miss first tr., 1 tr. into next tr., * leaving the last loop of each
on hook, 1 tr. into same st. as last tr., 1 tr. into next tr. (3 loops
on hook), w.o.h. and draw through all loops on hook (twin
treble made); **. Repeat from * to ** 8 times more, 3 tr. into next
tr., 1 tr. into next tr. Repeat from * to ** 12 times, 3 tr. into next
tr.; 1 tr. into next tr. Repeat from * to ** 22 times, 3 tr. into next
tr.; 1 tr. into next tr. Repeat from * to ** 12 times, 3 tr. into next
tr.; 1 tr. into next tr. Repeat from * to ** 10 times working last
tr. into turning ch., 3 ch., turn.
3rd row:
Miss first tr., 1 tr. into each of next 11 tw. tr., 3 tr. into next tr.,
1 tr. into each of next 15 tw. tr., 3 tr. into next tr., 1 tr. into each
of next 24 tw. tr., 3 tr. into next tr., 1 tr. into each of next 15
tw. tr., 3 tr. into next tr., 1 tr. into each of next 11 tw. tr., 1 tr.
into turning ch., 3 ch., turn.
4th row:
Twin tr. row (tw. tr.). Miss first tr., 1 tr. into next tr., 11 tw. tr.,
3 tr. into next tr., 1 tr. into next tr., 16 tw. tr., 3 tr. into next
tr., 1 tr. into next tr., 25 tw. tr., 3 tr. into next tr., 1 tr. into next

tr., 16 tw. tr., 3 tr. into next tr., 1 tr. into next tr., 12 tw. tr.
working last tr. into turning ch., 3 ch., turn.
5th row:
Tr. row. Miss first tr., 1 tr. into each of next 13 tr., 3 tr. into next
tr., 1 tr. into each of next 19 tr., 3 tr. into next tr., 28 tr., 3 tr.
into next tr., 19 tr., 3 tr. into next tr., 13 tr., 1 tr. into turning
ch., 3 ch., turn.
Continue in this way having 8 more trs. on each row for a further
6 rows.
Next row:
Miss first tr., 1 tr. into next tr., 19 tw. tr., 3 tr. into next tr., 1
tr. into next tr., 32 tw. tr., 3 tr. into next tr., 1 tr. into next tr.,
41 tw. tr., 3 tr. into next tr., 1 tr. into next tr., 32 tw. tr., 3 tr.
into next tr., 1 tr. into next tr., 19 tw. tr., 1 tr. into turning ch.
2 ch., turn.

Skirt

1st row:
Into 2nd tr. work 1 dc., pull up loop on hook to $\frac{1}{2}$ inch in height.
* insert hook into same tr., w.o.h. and pull loop through, w.o.h.
and draw through 1 loop on hook (chain stitch—ch. st. made),
pull up loop to $\frac{1}{2}$ inch. Repeat from * 4 times (6 loops on hook).
Insert hook once more into same tr., w.o.h. and pull loop
through, w.o.h. and draw through 1 loop on hook, but do not
pull this loop up. Slip the 6 loops off back end of hook leaving
the last ch. st. on hook (the 6 loops will be picked up on the
following row). Pull this ch. st. tightly, 2 ch. ** into next tr. work
1 dc. and pull up loop to $\frac{1}{2}$ inch. (1 ch. st. into same tr. and pull
up loop as before) 5 times (6 loops on hook), 1 ch. st. into same
tr. Slip the 6 loops off back end of hook leaving the last ch. st.
on hook, pulling it tightly, 2 ch., ** repeat from ** to ** into each
of next 2 tr. (miss 2 tr., repeat from ** to ** into each of next 4
tr.) 3 times. (16 grps. of loops to armhole.) Miss 35 tr. for
armhole and repeat from ** to ** into each of next 4 tr. (miss
2 tr., repeat from ** to ** into each of next 4 tr.) 7 times. (32
grps. along front.) Miss 35 tr. for armhole and repeat from ** to
** into each of next 4 tr. (miss 2 tr., and repeat from ** to **
into each of next 4 tr.), 3 times, (16 grps. from armhole.) 64 grps.
all round, turn.

2nd row:

1 sl. st. into each of first 3 loops, 3 ch., * sl. st. into each of next
2 loops, insert hook into last loop of grp. and into the first loop
of next grp. w.o.h. and draw through 3 loops on hook (2 loops
sl. st'd together), sl. st. into each of next 2 loops, 3 ch. Repeat
from * ending with sl. st. into each of last 3 loops, 2 ch., turn.

3rd row:

1 dc. into 3 ch. space of first grp. and pull up loop to ½ inch,
* 1 ch. st. into same space and pull up loop. Repeat from * 4
times more (6 loops on hook), 1 ch. st. into same 3 ch. space, pull
loop tightly. Slip the 6 loops off back end of hook leaving the last
ch. st. on hook, 2 ch. ** dc. into 3 ch. space of next grp. and
pull up loop (1 ch. st. into same space and pull up loop), 5 times
(6 loops on hook), 1 ch. st. into same space; slip the 6 loops off
back end of hook leaving the last ch. st. on hook, 2 ch. Repeat
from ** to end of row, turn.

Work 2nd and 3rd rows once more, then 2nd row ending with:
insert hook into last loop of grp. and into first loop of previous
row, w.o.h. and draw through 3 loops, thus closing the back of
robe, 3 ch., turn.

Now work 3rd and 2nd rows alternately joining rows together on
each 2nd round until 25 pattern rows have been worked or until
work measures 15 ins. from neck edge.

Next row:

Without turning and with wrong side of work facing, work in twin
tr. thus:

Sl. st. back in between grps., 3 ch., leaving the last loop of each
on hook. 1 tr. between grps., 1 tr. into next 3 ch. space, w.o.h.
and draw through 3 loops on hook; * twin tr. into same 3 ch.
space, 1 tr. into same 3 ch. space and 1 tr. between next 2 grps.,
w.o.h. and draw through 3 loops on hook, 1 tr. between same
grps, and 1 tr. into next 3 ch. space, w.o.h. and draw through 3
loops on hook. Repeat from * to end, join with sl. st., 3 ch., turn.

Next row:

1 tr. into each tw. tr. increasing 4 tr. evenly along the round, join
with sl. st., 3 ch., turn.

Next row:

Twin tr. row; join with sl. st., 3 ch., turn.

Next row:

1 tr. into each tw. tr. increasing 5 tr. evenly along the round, join
with sl. st., 3 ch., turn.

Next row:
Twin tr. row, join with sl. st., 2 ch., turn.
Next row:
Group pattern row: Work 1 grp. into first tw. tr., 2 ch. * miss
2 tw. tr., 1 grp into next tw. tr. 2 ch. Repeat from * to end, join
with sl. st., 2 ch., turn.
Next row:
Repeat 2nd row of skirt, join to first grp. of previous row, 2 ch.,
turn. Work in grp. pattern until 7 rounds of grps. have been
completed, 3 ch., turn. Beginning with wrong side facing, repeat
the 5 rows of tw. tr. and tr. increasing 4 tr. on the first tr. round
and 5 tr. on second tr. round, 2 ch., turn. Now work in grp.
pattern until 5 rounds of grps. have been completed, 3 ch., turn.
Next round. With wrong side facing, finish skirt with 1 round of
tw. tr. Fasten off.

Sleeves
Work round armholes for 2 complete rounds of grps., having 12
grps. on each sleeve., 3 ch.
Next round:
With wrong side facing, finish sleeve with 1 round tw. tr. Fasten
off.

COAT
Beginning at neck. Make 72 chain.
1st row:
Into 3rd ch. from hook work 1 grp. of loops; 2 ch., 1 tr. into
each of next 10 ch., 2 ch., 1 grp. into next ch., 2 ch., 1 tr.
into each of next 11 ch., 2 ch., 1 grp. into next ch., 2 ch., 1 tr.
into each of next 22 ch., 2 ch., 1 grp. into next ch., 2 ch., 1 tr.
into each of next 11 ch., 2 ch., 1 grp. into next ch., 2 ch., 1 tr.
into each of next 10 ch., 2 ch., 1 grp. into last ch., 2 ch., turn.
2nd row:
** 1 sl. st. into each of first 3 loops of grp., 3 ch., 1 sl. st. into
each of next 3 loops, 2 ch., ** 1 tr. into first tr., * leaving the
last loop of each on hook, 1 tr. into same st. as last tr., 1 tr. into
next tr. (3 loops on hook), w.o.h. and draw through all loops on
hook (twin tr.). Repeat from * 8 times more, 1 tr. into 2 ch. space,
2 ch. Repeat from ** to **, 1 tr. into next 2 ch. space, 1 tr. into
next tr. Repeat from * to * 10 times, 1 tr. into 2 ch., space, 2

ch. Repeat from ** to **, 1 tr. into 2 ch. space, 1 tr. into next
tr. Repeat from * to * 21 times. 1 tr. into 2 ch. space, 2 ch. Repeat
from ** to **, 1 tr. into 2 ch. space, 1 tr. into next tr. Repeat
from * to * 10 times, 1 tr. into 2 ch. space, 2 ch. Repeat from
** to **, 1 tr. into 2 ch. space, 1 tr. into next tr. Repeat from
* to * 8 times, 1 tr. into next tr., 2 ch. Repeat from ** to ** into
last grp. 2 ch., turn.

3rd row:

Work 1 grp. of loops into 3 ch. space of previous row, 2 ch., 1
tr. into each of next 11 tr., 1 tr. into 2 ch. space (12 tr. on front).
2 ch., 1 grp. into 3 ch. space of next grp., 2 ch., 1 tr. into 2 ch.
space, 1 tr. into each of next 13 tr., 1 tr. into 2 ch. space (15 tr.
or shoulder). 2 ch., grp. into 3 ch. space of next grp., 2 ch., 1
tr. into 2 ch. space, 1 tr. into each of next 24 tr., 1 tr. into 2 ch.
space (26 tr. on back). 2 ch., grp. into 3 ch. space of next grp.,
2 ch., 1 tr. into 2 ch. space, 1 tr. into each of next 13 tr., 1 tr.
into 2 ch. space (15 tr. on shoulder). 2 ch., grp. into 3 ch. space
of next grp., 2 ch., 1 tr. into 2 ch. space, 1 tr. into each of next
11 tr. (12 tr. on front). 2 ch., grp. into 3 ch. space of last grp.,
2 ch., turn.

Repeat the last 2 rows (1 row tw. tr. and 1 row tr. with grps. over
grps.), increasing 1 tr. each side of grps. (except on front edges)
or every row until 12 rows have been worked ending with twin tr.
row, 2 ch., turn. There should now be 21 tw. tr. on each front,
33 tw. tr. on each shoulder and 44 tw. tr. on back.

Armhole shaping

1 grp. into 3 ch. space of first grp., 2 ch., 21 tr., 2 ch., grp. into
3 ch. space of next grp., 10 ch., miss 33 tw. tr., grp. into 3 ch.
space of next grp., 2 ch., 1 tr. into 2 ch. space, 44 tr., 1 tr. into
2 ch. space, 2 ch., grp. into 3 ch. space of next grp., 10 ch., miss
33 tw. tr., grp. into 3 ch. space of next grp., 2 ch., 21 tr., 2 ch.,
grp. into 3 ch. space of last grp., 2 ch., turn.

Next row:

Sl. st. into each of first 3 loops, 3 ch., sl. st. into each of next
3 loops of grp. 2 ch., 21 tw. tr., 2 ch., sl. st. into each of next
3 loops, 3 ch., sl. st. into each of next 3 loops of grp., 2 ch., tw.
tr. into 10 ch. at armhole, 2 ch., sl. st. into each of 3 loops, 3
ch., sl. st. into each of next 3 loops of grp., 2 ch., tw. tr. into
46 tr. of back, 2 ch., sl. st. into next 3 loops, 3 ch., sl. st. into

next 3 loops of grp., 2 ch., tw. tr. into 10 ch. of armhole, 2 ch.,
sl. st. into each of next 3 loops, 3 ch., sl. st. into next 3 loops
of grp., 2 ch., tw. tr. into 21 tr., 2 ch., sl. st. into next 3 loops,
3 ch., sl. st. into next 3 loops of grp., 2 ch., turn.
Continue working straight in pattern keeping grps. over grps.
until 23 rows have been worked from armhole or work measures
approx. 8½ ins. from neck edge.
Next row:
1 grp. into 3 ch. space of first grp., 2 ch., 1 grp. into first tr.,
2 ch. (miss 2 tr., 1 grp. into next tr., 2 ch.), 6 times, miss 1 tr., 1
grp. into next tr., 2 ch., grp. into 3 ch. space of next grp.; 2 ch.,
1 grp. into next tr., 2 ch. (miss 2 tr., 1 grp. into next tr., 2 ch.),
3 times, grp. into 3 ch. space of next grp.; 2 ch., 1 grp. into next
tr., 2 ch. (miss 2 tr., 1 grp. into next tr., 2 ch.), 15 times, grp.
into 3 ch. space of next grp.; 2 ch., 1 grp. into next tr., 2 ch.
(miss 2 tr., 1 grp. into next tr., 2 ch.), 3 times, 1 grp. into 3 ch.
space of next grp., 2 ch. 1 grp. into next tr., 2 ch., miss 1 tr.,
1 grp. into next tr., 2 ch., (miss 2 tr., 1 grp. into next tr., 2 ch.)
6 times, 1 grp. into 3 ch. space of last grp., 2 ch., turn.
Next row:
Repeat 2nd row of skirt (sl. st. row), 2 ch., turn.
Next row:
1 grp. into 3 ch. space of first grp., 2 ch., * 1 grp. into 3 ch. space
of next grp., 2 ch. Repeat from * to end, turn.
Next row:
Repeat 2nd row of skirt (sl. st. row), 3 ch., turn.
Next row:
Repeat last row of skirt (twin tr. row). Fasten off.

Sleeves

With right side of work facing, work 46 tr. round armhole, join
with sl. st. 3 ch., turn.
Work in rounds of twin tr. and tr. alternately, joining each round
with sl. st. to turning ch. until 12 rounds have been worked
ending with twin tr. round, 2 ch., turn.
Next round:
Work 12 grps. evenly round sleeve end, 2 ch., turn.
Next round:
As 2nd row of skirt (sl. st. round), join with sl. st. Fasten off.

Neck edgings

For robe and coat.
Make 3 ch., join with sl. st. to form a circle.
1st row:
2 ch., work 1 grp. into circle, 2 ch., turn.
2nd row:
Sl st. into each of first 3 loops of grp., 3 ch., sl. st. into next 3
loops, 2 ch., turn.
3rd row:
1 grp. into 3 ch. space, 2 ch., turn.
Repeat last 2 rows for length required ending with 2nd row.
Fasten off.
Sew around each neck line.
Sew buttons on back of yoke on robe using the tr. ends as
buttonholes.
Press robe and coat *very lightly* under a slightly damp cloth.
Thread ribbon through one space at each front edge of coat,
make a small bow and let ribbon hang to lower edge of robe
(optional).

Crochet stitch sampler

MATERIALS

Double Crepe Wool 1 oz. Crochet hook size 3.50 (U.S. E).
Alternatively 1 40-gr. ball of synthetic yarn could be used.

METHOD

Make 40 chain.

1st row:

1 tr. into 4th ch. from hook, 1 tr. into each ch. to end, 3 ch.,
turn. (38 trs.)

2nd row:

Miss first tr., 1 tr. into each tr., 1 tr. into turning ch., 3 ch., turn.

3rd row:

Popcorn stitch: Miss first tr., 1 tr. into next tr., * 1 ch., 5 tr. into
next tr., drop loop from hook and insert hook into the 1 ch.,
space preceding the 5 tr. and draw loop of 5th tr. through
(popcorn st.), 1 tr. into each of next 2 tr. Repeat from * to end
working last tr. into turning ch., 1 ch., turn. (12 popcorn sts.)

4th row:

1 dc. into each st., 1 dc. into turning ch., 1 ch., turn. (38 dc.)

5th row:

1 dc. into each dc. to end, 1 ch., turn.

6th row:

As 5th row ending with 3 ch., turn.

7th row:

Crossed treble: Miss 2 dc., 1 tr. into next dc., working from behind,
1 tr. into last dc. missed (crossed tr.) * miss next dc., 1 tr. into
next dc., working from behind, 1 tr. into last dc. missed (another
cross tr. made). Repeat from * to within last dc., 1 tr. into last
dc., 3 ch., turn.

8th row:

Miss first 2 tr., 1 tr. into next tr., working from behind, 1 tr. into

last tr. missed (cross tr. made over cross tr.). * cross tr. over next
cross tr. Repeat from * ending with 1 tr. into top of turning ch.,
4 ch., turn. (18 cross tr.)

9th row:

Spaces: Miss first 2 tr., 1 tr. into next tr., * 1 ch., miss 1 tr., 1
tr. into next tr. Repeat from * working last tr. into turning ch.
1 ch., turn. (19 spaces.)

10th row:

1 dc. into first space, * 3 ch., miss (1 tr., 1 space and 1 tr.) and
work 1 dc. into next space, 1 dc. into tr., 1 dc. into next space.
Repeat from * ending with 3 ch., 1 dc. into last space, 1 dc. into
turning ch., 2 ch., turn.

11th row:

This and the following 3 rows are a combination of (ch., dc., tr.,
dbl. tr.). * Miss first dc., 1 dc. into next dc. (2 tr., 3 dbl. tr. and
2 tr.), into 3 ch. loop. Repeat from * ending with 1 dc. into each
of last 2 dc., 3 ch., turn.

12th row:

Miss 2 dc. and 2 tr. and work 1 dc. into each of next 3 dbl. tr.
* 3 ch., 1 dc. into each of 3 dbl. tr. of next group. Repeat from
* ending with 1 dbl. tr. into last dc., 4 ch., turn.

13th row:

1 dbl. tr. and 2 tr. into first space, miss 1 dc. of grp., 1 dc. into
next dc., * (2 tr., 3 dbl. tr. and 2 tr.) into next 3 ch. space, miss
1 dc., 1 dc. into next dc. Repeat from * ending with 2 tr., and
1 dbl. tr. into last space, 1 dbl. tr. into turning ch., 2 ch., turn.

14th row:

1 dc. into each of first 2 dbl. tr., * 3 ch., 1 dc. into each of 3
dbl. tr. of next grp.; repeat from * ending with 1 dc. into last dbl.
tr., 1 dc. into turning ch., 4 ch., turn.

15th row:

Spaces: Miss first dc., 1 tr. into next dc., 1 ch., 1 tr. into first space,
* 1 ch., 1 tr. into first dc. of next grp., 1 ch., miss 1 dc., 1 tr.
into next dc., 1 ch., 1 tr. into next space. Repeat from * ending
with 1 ch., 1 tr. into next dc., 1 ch., 1 tr. into last dc. 2 ch., turn.

16th row:

Half treble: 1 hlf. tr. into first space, hlf. tr. into tr., * hlf. tr. into
next space, hlf. tr., into tr. Repeat from * working last hlf. tr. into
turning ch., 2 ch., turn.

17th row:
1 hlf. tr. between the first two half. trs., 1 hlf. tr. between each
hlf. tr. to end, 2 ch., turn.
18th row:
As 17th row, 4 ch., turn.
19th row:
3-treble cluster: Miss first hlf. tr., holding back the last loop of each
or hook, work 3 tr. into next st. (4 loops on hook), w.o.h. and
draw through all loops on hook (cluster made), 1 ch., * miss next
hlf. tr., cluster into next st., 1 ch. Repeat from * ending with 1
tr. into turning ch., 1 ch., turn. (18 clusters.)
20th row:
2 dc. into space preceding first cluster, * 2 dc. into next 1 ch.
space. Repeat from * to end, 4 ch., turn. (38 dc.)
21st row:
Double treble: Miss first dc., 1 dbl. tr. into each dc. to end, 1 ch.,
turn.
22nd row:
1 dc. into each dbl. tr., 1 dc. into turning ch., 4 ch., turn.
23rd row:
Crossed dbl. tr: Miss 2 dcs., 1 dbl. tr. into next dc., working from
behind, 1 dbl. tr. into last dc. missed, * miss 1 dc., 1 dbl. tr. into
next dc., working from behind, 1 dbl. tr. into last dc. missed.
Repeat from * to within last dc., 1 dbl. tr. into last dc., 1 ch.,
turn.
24th row:
1 dc. into each dbl. tr. 1 dc. into turning ch., 4 ch., turn.
25th row:
Dbl. tr. cluster pattern: Holding back the last loop of each on hook,
work 3 dbl. tr. into 2nd dc. (4 loops on hook) w.o.h. and draw
through all loops on hook ($\frac{1}{2}$ group made), miss 4 dc., * holding
back the last loop of each on hook, 3 dbl. tr. into next dc. (4
loops on hook) w.o.h. and draw through all loops on hook, 4 ch.,
3 dbl. tr. into same dc. as last $\frac{1}{2}$ group, w.o.h. and draw through
all loops on hook (1 whole group made), miss 4 dc. Repeat from
* ending with $\frac{1}{2}$ group into next dc., 1 dbl. tr. into turning ch.,
4 ch., turn.
26th row:
1 whole group into top of first $\frac{1}{2}$ group, * miss 4 ch., 1 whole
grp., between the next 2 whole grps. of previous row: Repeat

from * ending with dbl. tr. into turning ch., 3 ch., turn.
27th row:
* 3 tr. over 4 ch. space, 2 tr. into space between grps. Repeat from
* ending with 3 tr. over next 4 ch., 1 tr. into turning ch., 3 ch.,
turn.
28th row:
Twin treble: Miss first tr., 1 tr. into next tr. * holding back the last
loop of each on hook, 1 tr. into same st. as last tr., 1 tr. into next
tr. (3 loops on hook) w.o.h. and draw through all loops on hook,
(twin tr. made). Repeat from * working last tr. into turning ch.,
3 ch., turn.
29th row:
Miss first twin tr., 1 tr. into each twin tr., 1 tr. into turning ch.,
3 ch., turn.
30th row:
Pine stitch: Miss first tr., * (w.o.h., insert hook into next tr. and
pull up loop to $\frac{1}{2}$ inch in height) 4 times (9 loops on hook), w.o.h.
and draw through all loops on hook (pine st. made), 2 ch., miss
1 tr. Repeat from * ending with 1 tr. into turning ch., 3 ch., turn.
31st row:
1 tr. into space preceding first pine st., * 2 tr. into next space
between pine sts. Repeat from * ending with 1 tr. into last space,
1 tr. into turning ch., turn omitting a turning ch.
32nd row:
Sl. st. into each tr. (not tightly). Fasten off.
Turn work to lower edge and finish with a picot border as
follows:
With right side of work facing, rejoin wool and work into
foundation ch. * 3 ch., 1 dc. into 3rd ch. from hook, miss 1
foundation ch., sl. st. into next ch. Repeat from * to end. Fasten
off.
Press lightly on wrong side omitting popcorn groups.

Crochet square for bedspread 1

(To fit single bed).

MATERIALS
40 Hanks Twilley's No. 1. Health Vest Cotton. Crochet hook size 3.50 (U.S. E). Daisy Winder—obtainable with instructions enclosed at most wool shops.

Measurement of square
11 inches.

METHOD
Popcorn stitch (pc. st.): Work 3 or 4 tr. into 1 tr. or space as specified in pattern, drop loop from hook, insert hook into the chain preceding the trs. and draw dropped loop through.
Decreasing in treble: Work off 2 tr. as 1 tr. thus: * W.o.h., draw a loop through next tr. (3 loops on hook) w.o.h. and draw through 2 loops. (2 loops on hook.) Repeat from * once more (3 loops on hook) w.o.h. and draw through all loops on hook. (1 tr. decreased.)
Make 54 squares and 2 half-squares.
Begin at centre of square by making a double petal daisy.
1st round:
Join cotton to any double petal with a sl. st. and work * 3 ch., sl. st. into next dbl. petal. Repeat from * all round, sl. st. into first 3 ch. space between petals.
2nd round:
4 ch., 3 tr. into space, drop loop from hook, insert hook into the 4th of 4 starting ch. and draw dropped loop through (pc. st.), 2 ch., 4-tr. pc. st. into same space, 2 ch., * into next space between petals work (4-tr. pc. st., 2 ch., 4-tr. pc. st.), 2 ch. Repeat from

* all round, join with sl. st. into space between first 2 pc. sts. (24 pc. sts.—2 into each space.)

3rd round:
4 ch. (counts as first tr. in 4-tr. pc. st., 5 ch., 4-tr. pc. st.), into same space (corner) 2 ch., 3 tr. into next space between pc. sts. 2 tr. into each of next 3 spaces between pc. sts., 3 tr. into next space 3 ch., * into next corner work (4-tr. pc. st., 5 ch., 4-tr. pc. st.) 2 ch., 3 tr. into next space, 2 tr. into each of next 3 spaces, 3 tr. into next space, 3 ch. Repeat from * all round, join with sl. st. into 5 ch. space at corner. (12 tr. on each side of square.)

4th round:
* (4-tr. pc. st., 5 ch., 4-tr. pc. st.) into corner space, 3 ch., 3-tr. pc. st. into 2 ch. space, 2 ch., dec. 1 tr., 1 tr. into each of next 8 tr. dec. 1 tr., 3 ch., 3-tr. pc. st. into space, 3 ch. Repeat from * ending with sl. st. into 5 ch. space at corner.

5th round:

* (4-tr. pc. st., 5 ch., 4-tr. pc. st.) into corner, (3 ch., 3-tr. pc. st.
into next space) twice, 2 ch., dec. 1 tr., 1 tr. into each of next 6
tr., dec. 1 tr. (3 ch., 3-tr. pc. st. into next space), twice, 3 ch.
Repeat from * ending with sl. st. into 5 ch. space at corner.
Repeat the 5th round working one more 3-tr. pc. st. on each side
of corner and at the same time dec. 1 tr. at each side of trs. on
every round for 4 more rounds. (6 3-tr. pc. sts., 1 tr. and 6 3-tr.
pc. sts. on each side of square.)

Next round:

* Work 5 dc. into 5 ch. space at corner (2 dc. into space, 1 dc.
into ch. over pc. st.), 6 times, 2 dc. into next space, 1 dc. into
tr. (2 dc. into space, 1 dc. into ch. over pc. st.) 6 times, 2 dc. into
next space. Repeat from * join with sl. st. Fasten off.

Half-square

Make a double petal daisy.
Join cotton to any double petal with sl. st. and work, * 3 ch., sl.
st. into next dbl. petal. Repeat from * 6 times more.
(7 spaces between petals.) Break off cotton.

2nd row:

Join cotton into first 3 ch. space at beginning of row, 4 ch., 4-tr.
pc. st. into same space, 2 ch., * (4-tr. pc. st., 2 ch., 4-tr. pc. st.)
into next 3 ch. space, 2 ch. Repeat from * 4 times more, 4-tr. pc.
st. into next 3 ch. space, 1 ch., 1 tr. into same space. Break off
cotton.

3rd row:

Rejoin cotton into 1 ch. space preceding the first pc. st., 4 ch.,
4-tr. pc. st. into same space, 2 ch., 3 tr. into next space, 2 tr. into
each of next 3 spaces, 3 tr., into next space, 3 ch. (4-tr. pc. st.,
5 ch., 4-tr. pc. st.), into next space (corner), 2 ch., 3 tr. into next
space, 2 tr. into each of next 3 spaces, 3 tr. into next space, 3
ch., 4-tr. pc. st. into 1 ch. space, 1 ch., 1 tr. into same space.
Break off cotton.

4th row:

Rejoin cotton into 1 ch. space, 4 ch., 4-tr. pc. st. into same space,
3 ch., 3-tr. pc. st. into 2 ch. space, 2 ch., dec. 1 tr., 1 tr. into
each of next 8 tr., dec. 1 tr., 3 ch., 3-tr. pc. st. into space, 3 ch.
(4-tr. pc. st., 5 ch., 4-tr. pc. st.), into corner, 3 ch., 3-tr. pc. st.
into space, 2 ch., dec. 1 tr., 1 tr. into each of next 8 tr., dec. 1

tr., 3 ch., 3-tr. pc. st. into space, 3 ch., 4-tr. pc. st. into 1 ch.
space, 1 ch., 1 tr. into same space. Break off cotton.
5th row:
Rejoin cotton into 1 ch. space, 4 ch., 4-tr. pc. st. into same space,
(3 ch., 3-tr. pc. st. into next space), twice, 2 ch., dec. 1 tr., 1 tr.
into each of next 6 tr., dec. 1 tr. (3 ch., 3-tr. pc. st. into next
space), twice, 3 ch. (4-tr. pc. st., 5 ch., 4-tr. pc. st.), into corner
(3 ch., 3-tr. pc. st. into next space), twice, 2 ch., dec. 1 tr., 1 tr.
into each of next 6 tr., dec. 1 tr. (3 ch., 3-tr. pc. st. into next
space), twice, 3 ch., 4-tr. pc. st. into 1 ch. space, 1 ch., 1 tr. into
same space. Break off cotton.

Repeat the 5th row working one more 3-tr. pc. st. etc. as for
square with 4-tr. pc. st. at each end, 4 times more.
Weave all loose ends in neatly on wrong side of work.
With right side of work facing, join cotton with sl. st. into first
free petal of daisy. * 3 ch., sl. st. into next petal. Repeat from *
3 times, 3 ch., 3 dc. into space of first pc. st. (3 dc. into space
of pc. st. at each row end), 6 times, ** 5 dc. into corner (3 dc. into
space between pc. sts), 6 times, 2 dc. into next space, 1 dc. into
tr., 2 dc. into next space (3 dc. into space between pc. sts.), 6
times. Repeat from ** to next corner, 5 dc. into corner, 3 dc. into
each row end, 3 dc. into each 3 ch. of daisy, sl. st. into first dc.
Fasten off.

Joining of squares
Sew squares together on right side of work catching the outside
loop of each dc. Turn to wrong side and sew along the remaining
loops of dc.

Edging
Join cotton to corner and work, * 5 ch., 2 dbl. tr. into 5th ch.
from hook, miss 3 dc., sl. st. into next dc. Repeat from * all
round. Fasten off.

Crochet square for bedspread 2

(To fit single bed).

MATERIALS
Approx. 40 hanks Twilley's No. 1 Health Vest Cotton. Crochet hook size 4.00 (U.S. F). Daisy winder—obtainable at most wool shops with instructions enclosed.

Measurement of square
11 ins.

METHOD
Make 54 squares and 2 half-squares.
Start with centre of square by making a double petal daisy.
1st round:
Join cotton to any double petal and work thus: 3 ch., leaving the last loop of each on hook work 2 tr. into petal (3 loops on hook), w.o.h. and draw through all loops on hook (cluster made), 3 ch., leaving the last loop of each on hook, 3 tr. into same petal (4 loops on hook), w.o.h. and draw through all loops on hook (another cluster), 2 ch., 2 tr. into each of next 2 dbl. petals, 2 ch., * into next dbl. petal work (1 cluster, 3 ch., 1 cluster), 2 ch., 2 tr. into each of next 2 dbl. petals, 2 ch. Repeat from * all round, sl. st. to top of first cluster.
2nd round:
Sl. st. into 3 ch. space between clusters * (cluster, 3 ch., cluster) into same space, 2 ch., 2 tr. into 2 ch. space, 1 tr. into each of 4 tr., 2 tr. into 2 ch. space, 2 ch. Repeat from * ending with sl. st. into top of first cluster.
Work a further 4 rounds having 2 more trs. on each side of the trs. between clusters.
There should now be 24 tr. on each side of square.

7th round:

Sl. st. into space between clusters, ** (cluster, 3 ch., cluster) into 3 ch. space, 2 ch., 2 tr. into 2 ch. space, miss 1 tr., * 1 ch., 5 tr. into next tr., drop loop from hook, insert hook into the 1 ch. space preceding the 5 tr. and draw dropped loop through (popcorn st.). 1 ch., 1 tr. into each of next 2 tr. Repeat from * 6 times more, 1 ch., popcorn st. into next tr., miss 1 tr., 2 tr. into 2 ch. space. Repeat from ** all round, sl. st. to top of cluster (8 popcorn sts. on each side of square).

8th round:

** (cluster, 3 ch., cluster) into corner, 2 ch., 2 tr. into space, * 1 tr. into each of next 2 tr., 1 tr. into ch. at back of popcorn st. Repeat from * 7 times more, 1 tr. into each of next 2 tr., 2 tr. into space, 2 ch. Repeat from ** all round, sl. st. to top of cluster.

9th round:
* (cluster, 3 tr., cluster) into corner, 2 ch., 2 tr. into space, 1 tr. into each tr., 2 tr. into space, 2 ch. Repeat from * all round sl. st. to top of cluster. Fasten off. (34 trs. on each side of square.)

Half-square
Make a double daisy.
Join cotton to any double petal and work 3 ch., 3 tr. cluster into same petal, 2 ch., 2 tr. into each of next 2 dbl. petals, 2 ch. (cluster, 3 ch., cluster) into next dbl. petal, 2 ch., 2 tr. into each of next 2 dbl. petals, 2 ch., 1 cluster into next dbl. petal, 1 ch., 1 tr. into same petal. Break off cotton and rejoin into 1 ch. space at beginning of row.
Next row:
3 ch., 3 tr. cluster into same space, 2 ch., 2 tr. into 2 ch. space, 1 tr. into each of next 4 tr., 2 tr. into 2 ch. space, 2 ch. (cluster, 3 ch., cluster), into corner space, 2 ch., 2 tr. into space, 1 tr. into each of next 4 tr., 2 tr. into space, 2 ch., 1 cluster into 1 ch. space, 1 ch., 1 tr. into same space as cluster.

Break off cotton and rejoin into 1 ch. space at beginning of row. Work a further 4 rows having 2 more tr. each side of the trs. between clusters. (24 trs. on each side of half-square.)
7th row:
As 7th row of square having 1 cluster at each end of half-square.
8th row:
As 8th row of square having 1 cluster at each end.
9th row:
Join cotton into 1 ch. space at beginning of row, 1 cluster into same space, 2 ch., 2 tr. into space, 1 tr. into each tr., 2 tr. into space, 2 ch. (cluster, 3 ch., cluster), into corner, 2 ch., 2 tr. into space, 1 tr. into each tr., 2 tr. into space, 2 ch., 1 cluster into 1 ch space, working along lower edge of half-square (3 tr. into end of next cluster), 7 times, and into end of next cluster work 2 tr., 1 hlf. tr., then 1 dc. into first free dbl. petal of daisy, * 2 ch., 1 dc into next daisy petal. Repeat from * 3 times more, 1 hlf. tr. and 2 tr. into end of next cluster, 3 tr. into each cluster to end, sl. st. into cluster.
Fasten off.
Weave all loose ends in on wrong side of work.

Joining the squares

Sew squares together on right side of work catching the outside
loop of each tr.; then turn to wrong side and sew along the
remaining loops of trs. When 4 squares have been joined together,
work a centre thus:
1 cluster into each 3 ch. space, round centre and then 1 sl. st. into
each of the 4 clusters. Fasten off securely.
Finish bedspread with 2 rows of tr. all round and then working
from left to right 1 dc. into each tr. Fasten off.

Cushion cover

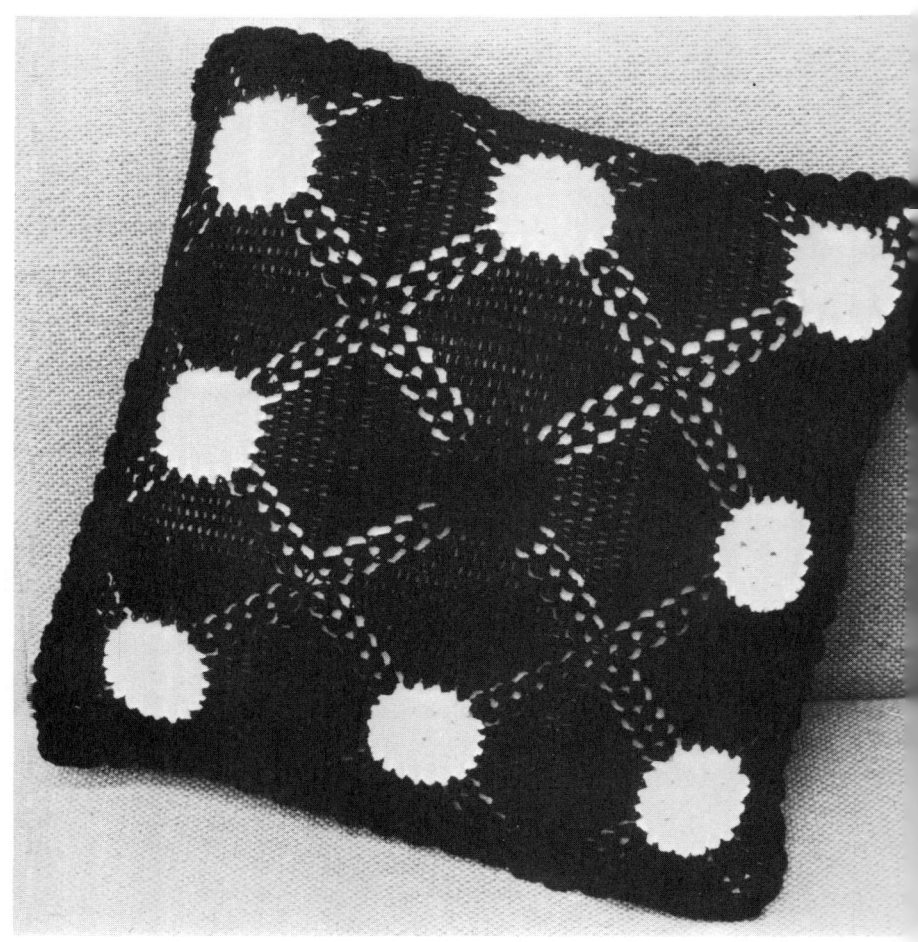

MATERIALS
5 balls Twilley's Lyscordet in black and 2 balls in white or colours
of your choice. Crochet hook size 2.50 (U.S. C). Zipper or snap
fasteners.

Measurement
14 ins. square.

METHOD
First side
Using black and beginning at centre of square, make 5 chain and
join with sl. st. to form a ring.

1st round:
4 ch., 3 tr. into ring, drop loop from hook, insert hook into 4th
of 4 starting ch. and draw dropped loop through (popcorn
stitch—pc. st. made). * 2 ch., 4 tr. into ring, drop loop from
hook, insert hook into 2 ch. space preceding 4 tr. and draw
dropped loop through (another pc. st. made). Repeat from * 3
times more, 2 ch., join with sl. st. to top of first pc. st. (5 pc. sts.)

2nd round:
Sl. st. into space between pc. sts. and work 4 ch., 3 tr. into same
space as sl. st. drop loop from hook, insert hook into 4th of 4
starting ch. and draw dropped loop through, 2 ch., pc. st. into
same space, 2 ch., * pc. st., 2 ch. and pc. st. into next space
between pc. sts., 2 ch. Repeat from * all round, join with sl. st.
to top of first pc. st. (10 pc. sts.)

3rd round:
Repeat 2nd round. (20 pc. sts.)

4th round:
Sl. st. into space, 3 ch. (to count as tr.) and leaving the last loop
of each on hook work 2 tr. into same space as sl. st., thread over
hook and draw through all loops on hook (3-tr. cluster made), 3
ch., leaving the last loop of each on hook work 3 tr. into same
space as last cluster, thread over hook and draw through all loops
on hook (another 3-tr. cluster made). * 2 ch., 2 tr. into each of
next 4 spaces between pc. sts., 2 ch., into next space work cluster,
3 ch. and cluster. Repeat from * all round joining last 2 ch. to
top of first cluster.

5th round:
Sl. st. into space, 3 ch. (to count as tr.) cluster, 3 ch. and cluster

into same space as sl. st., * 2 ch., 2 tr. into next space, 1 tr. into each of next 8 tr., 2 tr. into space, 2 ch., cluster, 3 ch. and cluster into next space (corner space). Repeat from * all round joining last 2 ch. to top of first cluster. (12 trs. on each side of square.) Work a further 3 rounds having 4 more tr. on each side of square in each round.

There should now be 24 tr. on each side of square. Fasten off. Make 8 more squares working the first 3 rounds in white. Break off white and join in black for remainder of square.

Joining squares
Having the black square in the centre of cushion, sew squares together on right side of work catching the outside loop of each tr. Turn work to wrong side and catch along the remaining loops of trs. Fasten off.

Second side
Using white work the first 3 rounds as for first side.
4th round:
Repeat 3rd round. (40 pc. sts.)
5th round:
Sl. st. into space, pc. st. into each space between pc. sts. (40 pc. sts.)
6th round:
Repeat 5th round. (40 pc. sts.) Break off white.
7th round:
Join in black with sl. st. into space between pc. sts. and work pc. st., 4 ch. and pc. st. into same space as sl. st. 2 ch., 2 tr. into each of next 4 spaces, 1 tr. into next space, 2 tr. into each of next 4 spaces, * 2 ch., pc. st., 4 ch. and pc. st. into next space (corner space), 2 ch., 2 tr. into each of next 4 spaces, 1 tr. into next space, 2 tr. into each of next 4 spaces. Repeat from * all round, 2 ch., join to top of first pc. st.
8th round:
Sl. st. into space, pc. st., 4 ch. and pc. st. into same space as sl. st. (corner space) 2 ch., 2 tr. into next space, 1 tr. into each of next 17 tr., 2 tr. into next space, * 2 ch., pc. st., 4 ch. and pc. st. into corner space, 2 ch., 2 tr. into space, 1 tr. into each of next 17 tr., 2 tr. into space. Repeat from * all round, 2 ch., join to top of first pc. st.

Work a further 7 rounds having 4 more trs. on each side of square in each round.

There should now be 49 trs. on each side of square.

16th round:
Sl. st. into space, * pc. st., 4 ch. and pc. st. into corner space, 2 ch., 2 tr. into space, 1 tr. into each of next 24 trs., pc. st. into next tr., 1 tr. into each of next 24 trs., 2 tr. into space, 2 ch. Repeat from * all round, join to top of first pc. st.

17th round:
Sl. st. into space, * pc. st., 4 ch. and pc. st. into corner space, 2 ch., 2 tr. into space, 25 tr., pc. st. into next tr., 1 tr. into pc. st. of previous round, pc. st. into next tr., 25 tr., 2 tr. into space, 2 ch. Repeat from * all round, join with sl. st.

18th round:
Sl. st. into space, * pc. st., 4 ch. and pc. st. into corner space, 2 ch., 2 tr. into space, 26 tr., 3 pc. sts. with 1 tr. between each pc. st., 26 tr., 2 tr. into space, 2 ch. Repeat from * all round, join with sl. st.

19th round:
Sl. st. into space, * pc. st., 4 ch. and pc. st. into corner, 2 ch., 2 tr. into space, 27 tr., 4 pc. sts. with 1 tr. between each pc. st., 27 tr., 2 tr. into space, 2 ch. Repeat from * all round, join with sl. st.

20th round:
Sl. st. into space, * pc. st., 4 ch. and pc. st. into corner, 2 ch., 2 tr. into space, 28 tr., 5 pc. sts. with 1 tr. between each pc. st., 28 tr., 2 tr. into space, 2 ch. Repeat from * all round, join with sl. st.

21st round:
Sl. st. into space, * pc. st., 4 ch. and pc. st. into corner, 2 ch., 2 tr. into space, 29 tr., 6 pc. sts. with 1 tr. between each pc. st., 29 tr., 2 tr. into space, 2 ch. Repeat from * all round, join with sl. st.

22nd round:
Sl. st. into space, * pc. st., 4 ch. and pc. st. into corner, 2 ch., 2 tr. into space, 73 tr., 2 tr. into space, 2 ch. Repeat from * all round, join with sl. st.

23rd round:
Sl. st. into space, * pc. st., 4 ch. and pc. st. into corner, 2 ch.,

2 tr. into space, 77 tr., 2 tr. into space, 2 ch. Repeat from * all round, join with sl. st.

Work 3 rows dc. along one side only for the purpose of closing cushion cover with snap fasteners.

Sew around three sides of cover as for squares.

Attach snap fasteners or zip fastener for closing.

Edging

Using black Lyscordet double with hook size 3.00 (U.S. D), work * 5 chain, 3 dbl. tr. cluster into 5th ch. from hook. Repeat from * until edging is long enough to fit round cushion, approx. 50 ins. Fasten off, leaving a length of cotton for adjustment if necessary. Press. Sew around edge of cover allowing scalloped edge to extend beyond edge of cushion.

Penguin finger plate

(Suitable for bathroom or nursery).

MATERIALS
A small quantity of Coats Mercer Crochet Cotton No. 10 in Black, White and Mid-Buttercup No. 442. Steel crochet hook size 1.25.

METHOD

Front
Using White and beginning at lower edge, make 15 chain.
1st row:
1 dc. into 2nd ch. from hook, 1 dc. into each of next 13 ch., 3 ch., turn.
2nd row:
Miss first dc., 1 tr. into each of next 12 dc., 2 tr. into last dc., 1 ch., turn.
3rd row:
1 dc. into each tr., 1 dc. into top of turning ch., 3 ch., turn.
4th row:
Miss first dc., 1 tr. into each dc. to end., 1 ch., turn.
5th row:
1 dc. into each tr., 1 dc. into top of turning ch., 3 ch., turn.
Repeat the last 2 rows once more.
8th row:
Miss first dc., leaving the last loop of each on hook, 1 tr. into each of next 2 dc., thread over hook and draw through all loops on hook, 1 tr. into each dc. to end., 1 ch., turn.
9th row:
1 dc. into each tr., 1 dc. into top of turning ch., 3 ch., turn.
Repeat the last 2 rows once more.

12th row:
Miss first dc., decrease 1 tr., 1 tr. into each dc. to within last 3
dc., dec. 1 tr., 1 tr. into last dc., 1 ch., turn.
13th row:
1 dc. into each tr., 1 dc. into top of turning ch., 3 ch., turn.
Repeat the last 2 rows 3 times more, omitting 3 turning ch. at end
of last row. Fasten off.

Flipper
Using Black and beginning at tip, make 3 ch.
1st row:
1 dc. into 2nd ch. from hook, 1 dc. into next ch., 1 ch., turn.
2nd row:
2 dc. into first dc., 1 dc. into next dc., 1 ch., turn.
3rd row:
1 dc. into each dc. to end, 1 ch., turn.
4th row:
2 dc. into first dc., 1 dc. into each st. to end, 1 ch., turn. Repeat
the last 2 rows until work measures 1 inch ending with 3rd row.
2 ch., turn.
Next row:
Miss first dc., 1 hlf. tr. into next dc., 1 dc. into each st. to end,
1 ch., turn.
Next row:
1 dc. into each st., 1 dc. into turning ch., 2 ch., turn. Repeat the
last 2 rows once more omitting turning ch. at end of last row.
Fasten off.

Back
Work as for flipper until work measures 1 inch, 1 ch., turn.
Next row:
2 dc. into first dc., 1 dc. into each dc. to within last 2 dc., dec.
1 dc., 1 ch., turn.
Next row:
1 dc. into each dc., 1 ch., turn. Repeat the last 2 rows until work
measures 3 inches, ending at front.

Neck and head shaping
1st row:
Decrease 1 dc., 1 dc. into each st. to within last 2 dc., dec. 1 dc.,
1 ch., turn.

2nd row:
1 dc. into each dc. to end., 3 ch., turn.
3rd row:
7 tr. into first dc., 1 ch., 1 dc. into last dc. of row, turn.
4th row:
1 dc. into 1 ch. space, 1 hlf. tr. into first tr., 1 tr. into next tr.,
2 tr. into each of next 4 tr., 1 hlf. tr. into next tr., 1 dc. into
turning ch. Fasten off.

Beak
Using Mid-Buttercup, make 8 chain and work 1 sl. st. into 2nd
ch from hook, 1 dc. into next ch., 1 hlf. tr. into each of next 2
ch , 1 tr. into each of next 3 ch. Fasten off.

Foot
Using Mid-Buttercup, make 2 chain.
1st row:
3 dc. into 2nd ch. from hook, 1 ch., turn.
2nd row:
2 dc. into first dc., 1 dc. into next dc., 2 dc. into next dc., 1 ch.,
turn.
3rd row:
2 dc. into first dc., 1 dc. into next 3 dc., 2 dc. into last dc., 1
ch , turn.
4th row:
2 dc. into first dc., 1 dc. into each of next 5 dc., 2 dc. into last
dc , 3 ch., turn.
5th row:
Leaving the last loop of each tr. on hook (miss 2 dc., 1 tr. into
next dc.) 3 times, thread over hook and draw through all loops
on hook, 1 ch., sl. st. into 3 turning ch. Fasten off.
Work a second foot to match.

To make up
Press each piece separately.
Cut a piece of cardboard to fit into finger plate. Cover cardboard
with material—a sea-green shade in colour. Assemble penguin by
sticking the pieces on to the covered cardboard using a good
adhesive.

Irish rose picture

The following three designs are not my own work but have been adapted from very old patterns which have been firm favourites of mine for many years. Since crochet for the home is once again becoming fashionable I wished to re-create them for, I hope, other people's pleasure.

MATERIALS
Coats Mercer Crochet Cotton No. 20—1 ball each of Ecru, shade No. 609. Spring Green, shade No. 623. Variegated Gold, shade No. 897. Steel crochet hook size 1.25.

METHOD
With Ecru.
Begin by making 7 chain, join with a sl. st. to form a ring.
1st round:
3 ch., 1 tr. into ring, 3 ch., * 2 tr. into ring leaving the last loop of each on hook (3 loops on hook), thread over hook, and draw through all loops at one time (2-tr. cluster), 3 ch. Repeat from * 6 times, join with sl. st. to 3rd of 3 ch.
2nd round:
1 ch., 4 dc. over each loop, join with sl. st.
3rd round:
8 ch., 1 tr. into same place as sl. st., miss 4 dc., * 1 tr., 5 ch., 1 tr. into space over next cluster stitch of previous round. Repeat from * all round, join with sl. st. into 3rd of 8 ch.
4th round:
1 ch., * 6 dc. over next loop, 1 dc. in centre of next trs. Repeat from * all round, join with sl. st.

5th round:

Sl. st. into each of next 2 dc., 18 ch., 1 dc. into 2nd ch. from
hook, work 19 dc. over rest of ch., 1 sl. st. into each of next 2
dc. of circle, ** 1 ch., turn and working in back loop of stitch only
for entire strip, 1 dc. into each of the next 19 dc. on strip, 3 ch.,
turn, 1 dc. into 3rd ch. from hook, 1 dc. into each of the next
5 dc. * 1 ch., turn, 1 dc. into each of next 4 dc., 3 ch., turn 1
dc. into 3rd ch. from hook, 1 dc. into each of next 4 dc., 1 dc.
into each of the next 2 dc. on side of strip. Repeat from * 6 times
more, 1 sl. st. into next 5 dc. of circle, working through both
loops, 17 ch., turn, sl. st. into 3rd picot from bottom of first strip,
1 ch., turn and work 20 dc. over chain, 1 sl. st. into each of next
2 dc. of circle (working through both loops). Repeat from ** until
7 strips have been completed.

Work another strip joining the 3rd picot from bottom to tip of
first strip made and complete strip, then work 1 sl. st. into each
of last 3 dc. of circle. Break off cotton.

6th round:

Join cotton to 2nd free picot of any strip, 1 dc. into same place,
** 6 ch., 1 dc. into next picot, * 6 ch., 1 dc. into next picot.
Repeat from * once more, 6 ch., miss first picot of next strip, 1
dc. into next picot. Repeat from ** 6 times, ending round with
* 6 ch., 1 dc. into next picot. Repeat from * twice, 2 ch., 1 dbl.
tr. into first dc.

7th round:

* 7 ch., 1 dc. into next loop. Repeat from * all round ending with
3 ch., 1 dbl. tr. into dbl. tr. of previous round.

8th round:

* 8 ch., 1 dc. into next loop. Repeat from * all round ending with
3 ch., 1 dbl. tr. into dbl. tr.

9th round:

* 9 ch., 1 dc. into next loop. Repeat from * all round ending with
3 ch., 1 triple tr. into dbl. tr.

10th round:

3 ch., 2 tr. into same space leaving the last loop of each on hook,
thread over hook and draw through all loops at one time (3 tr.
cluster). 5 ch., 3 tr. cluster into same space, * 7 ch., 1 dc. into
next loop, 7 ch., 3 tr. cluster, 5 ch., and 3 tr. cluster into next
loop. Repeat from * ending round with 7 ch., 1 dc. into next
loop, 7 ch., sl. st. into top of first cluster.

11th round:

Sl. st. into loop between cluster, 3 ch. (counts as first tr. of
cluster), and work 4 3-tr. clusters with 3 ch. between each cluster
into same loop, * 3 ch., 1 dc. into next loop, 7 ch., 1 dc. into
next loop, 3 ch., 4 cluster sets into next loop. Repeat from *
ending with 3 ch., 1 dc. into next loop, 7 ch., 1 dc. into next
loop, 3 ch., join with sl. st. into top of first cluster. Break off
cotton.

Pin out work and press using a damp cloth.

Roses

With Variegated Gold make 5 chain, join with sl. st. to form a
ring.

1st round:
6 ch., 1 tr. into ring, * 3 ch., 1 tr. into ring. Repeat from * 3
times, 3 ch., join with sl. st. to 3rd of 6 ch.
2nd round:
Over each loop, work 1 dc., 1 hlf. tr., 3 tr., 1 hlf. tr., and 1 dc.,
join with sl. st.
3rd round:
* 5 ch., 1 dc. into back of work between the dc. of next 2 petals.
Repeat from * all round.
4th round:
Over each loop, work 1 dc., 1 hlf. tr., 5 tr., 1 hlf. tr., and 1 dc.,
join with sl. st.
5th round:
* 6 ch., sl. st. into back of work between the next 2 petals. Repeat
from * all round.
6th round:
1 dc., 1 tr., 7 dbl. tr., 1 tr., 1 dc. into first loop, 1 dc., 1 tr., 4
dbl. tr. into next loop, 1 ch., sl. st. into 7 ch. loop between cluster
groups of circle (Ecru), 1 ch., sl. st. into 4th dbl. tr. on rose, 3
dbl. tr., 1 tr., 1 dc. into same loop on rose, * 1 dc., 1 tr., 7 dbl.
tr., 1 tr., 1 dc. into next loop. Repeat from *, join with sl. st.
Break off cotton. Make 7 more roses and join to 7 ch. loop
between alternate clusters.

Leaf
With Spring Green make 13 chain.
1 dc. into 2nd ch. from hook, 1 dc. into each of next 10 ch., 3
dc. into next ch. Working on other side of ch., work 1 dc. into
each of next 8 sts., 1 ch., turn. Picking up the back loop of each
stitch throughout, 1 dc. into each of the next 9 dc., 3 dc. into next
dc., 1 dc. into each of next 7 dc., * 1 ch. turn, 1 dc. into each
of next 8 dc., 3 dc. into next dc., 1 dc. into each of next 7 dc.
Repeat from * 4 times, 1 ch., turn, sl. st. into centre st. of 3rd
petal made of previous rose, 1 ch., turn, 1 dc. into each of next
8 dc., 2 dc. into next dc., 1 ch., sl. st. into next 7 ch. loop between
clusters on circle, 1 ch., 1 dc. into same st. on leaf, 1 dc. into each
of next 7 dc. on leaf, 1 ch., sl. st. into next petal of next rose,
1 ch., turn, sl. st. down side of leaf. Break off cotton. Make 7
more leaves and join in the same way.

Making up

With wrong side facing, place crochet on to ironing pad, place pins all round pulling into shape as you pin. Keep roses flat. Using a fairly hot iron and a very damp cloth, press. Leave crochet until thoroughly dry before extracting pins.

Cut a piece of cardboard $\frac{1}{2}$ in. larger in diameter than crochet.

Mark centre of cardboard. Cover cardboard with a circle of black velvet larger than cardboard and stick the edge down on the back with adhesive.

Place crochet on to mount, centre to centre. Pin out to within $\frac{1}{2}$ in. of outer edge of mount.

Sew to mount at centre of crochet and all round outer edge catching tips of leaves.

Have a frame made to your choice. This particular picture is framed in pewter.

Irish rose finger plate

MATERIALS

Crochet cotton and black velvet left over from 'Irish Rose' picture. Perspex finger plate.

METHOD

Work as given for pattern of roses and leaves in 'Irish Rose' picture. Cut a piece of cardboard to fit inside finger plate, cover with black velvet and stick roses and leaves on the velvet in a pattern to your own choice, using a good adhesive.

Plate doily

MATERIALS

The left-over cotton from the picture or—as in illustration—Coats
Mercer Crochet Cotton No. 20, Approx. ⅓ ball of white for centre,
⅓ ball Spring Green, shade No. 625 for leaves and small quantity
of Variegated Pink, shade No. 884 and Variegated Red, shade No.
885. Steel crochet hook, size 1.25. Pyrex plate 8 ins. in diameter.

METHOD

Beginning with centre, work as for picture for 7 rounds, ending
7th round with 1 ch., 1 triple tr. into dbl. tr.

8th round:
3 ch. (counts as first tr. of cluster), and work four 3-tr. clusters
with 3 ch. between each cluster into same loop, * 4 ch., 1 dc. into
next loop, 4 ch., 4 cluster sets into next loop. Repeat from *
ending with 4 ch., 1 dc. into next loop, 4 ch., sl. st. into top of
first cluster. Break off cotton.

Roses

Work as for rose in picture for 5 rounds.

6th round:
1 dc., 1 hlf. tr., 7 tr., 1 hlf. tr., 1 dc. into first loop, 1 dc., 1 hlf.
tr., 4 tr., into next loop, 1 ch., sl. st. into dc. between cluster grps.
of circle, 1 ch., sl. st. into 4th tr. on rose, 3 tr., 1 hlf. tr., 1 dc.
into same loop of rose, * 1 dc., 1 hlf. tr., 7 tr., 1 hlf. tr., 1 dc.
into next loop. Repeat from * join with sl. st.
Break off cotton. Make 7 more roses and join to dc. between
alternate cluster grps.

Leaf

With Spring Green make 11 chain.
1 dc. into 2nd ch. from hook, 1 dc. into each of next 8 ch., 3
dc. into next ch. Working on other side of chain, work 1 dc. into

each of next 7 dc., 1 ch., turn. Picking up the back loops of each st. throughout, 1 dc. into each of next 8 dc., 3 dc. into next dc., 1 dc. into each of next 6 dc., * 1 ch., turn, 1 dc. into each of next 7 dc., 3 dc. into next dc., 1 dc. into each of next 6 dc. Repeat from * 4 times, 1 ch., turn, sl. st. into centre st. of 3rd petal of previous rose, 1 ch., turn, 1 dc. into each of next 7 dc., 2 dc. into next dc., 1 ch., sl. st. into next dc. between cluster grps. 1 ch., 1 dc. into same st. on leaf, 1 dc. into each of next 6 dc., 1 ch., sl. st. into next petal of next rose, 1 ch., turn, sl. st. down side of leaf. Break off cotton. Make 7 more leaves and join in the same way.

Edge of plate

Join cotton (centre colour) to tip of any leaf, 1 dc. into same place, * 16 ch., 1 dc. into centre st. of rose, 16 ch., 1 dc. into tip of next leaf; repeat from * all round ending with sl. st. into first dc., 1 ch., turn.

Next round:

16 dc. over each chain loop, sl. st. into first dc., 1 ch., turn.

Next round:

1 dc. into each dc. all round, sl. st. to first dc. Break off cotton. Do not press. Attach to outer side of plate—see that rose petals are lying flat. Immerse plate in water and leave to dry.